Maude (age 78) and Agnes (age 75):
41 years together

Agnes: Actually, I don't see any difference in myself except that when I realize I'm seventy-five, I'm appalled. My mother was dead when she was seventy-five.

Maude: It's true that physical disabilities do get in the way. So that you can't . . . you don't . . . (she searches for a sufficiently genteel way to say this . . . and finds it) . . . you're not as limber as when you were younger. But that has nothing to do with what you would like to do or, you know. . . .

Susan: Do you intentionally do things with each other to be romantic? Is it something you're conscious of wanting to preserve in your relationship?

Maude: We never have done that, have we? We've not done things to feel romantic. That was one thing you used to tell me about your other friends, Agnes. They'd go in for all kinds of what I thought were very odd, official things, like gazing at the moon. Which I always thought was a lot of nonsense.

Susan: So it isn't as if you're wooing each other all the time?

Maude: No, that would be very tiresome, I would think. No, I just want to be as close to her as I always have been. Physically as close to her, and sex is part of it. I think that maybe some people begin to lose that feeling for contact. Would you suppose that's it?

Susan: It seems that they still have contact. It would be like, you know, sitting, watching TV, holding hands.

Agnes: Well, we only look at the news.

About the Author

Susan E. Johnson, Ph.D. (University of Wisconsin—Madison), has been a lesbian for thirty two years and a sociologist nearly as long. She has taught and conducted research at the University of Wisconsin— Madison, the University of Minnesota—Duluth, Rutgers University, and Antioch University—Seattle. Her research concentrates in the areas of sociology of mental health, sociology of law, and women's and lesbian studies. She has also worked and done research outside academic settings.

Susan lives with her partner in Seattle. She frequently gives lectures and workshops on the subject of long-term lesbian couples.

STAYING POWER:
LONG TERM LESBIAN COUPLES

by Susan E. Johnson

Learning Resources
Centre

The Naiad Press, Inc.
1994

Printed in the United States of America on acid-free paper
First Edition
Second Printing, August 1991
Third Printing, October 1994

Edited by Diane Benison
Cover design by Pat Tong and Bonnie Liss
    (Phoenix Graphics)
Typeset by Sandi Stancil

Library of Congress Cataloging-in-Publication Data

Johnson, Susan E., 1940–
    Staying power: long term lesbian couples / by Susan E. Johnson.
        p.   cm.
Includes bibliographical references.
    ISBN 0-941483-75-4
    1. Lesbian couples—United States—Case studies. I. Title.
HQ75.6.USJ64   1990
306.76'63—dc20
                                                                90-6254
                                                                    CIP

Acknowledgements

I have always felt that this project was the work of many women. This is my opportunity to acknowledge some of you. My utmost thanks go to:

Diane Benison, for her careful and thoughtful final editing of the manuscript;

Ruth Baetz, for a comprehensive, clear, and very gentle first editing;

Peg Cruikshank and Mary Denzel, for their sympathetic reading and helpful suggestions;

Sandra Jo Palm, for reading the manuscript, helping with fundraising, and telling me how much she wanted this book to exist;

Patricia Huling, for transcribing 2,500 pages of interviews with such accuracy and sensitivity that reading each interview was like being there again;

Lora Barnard, Sarah Draper, Susan Dyer, Joan Gottfried, Sylvia Harris, Anne Harvey, Dorothy Jones, Annette Lund, Jan Pickard, Barb Perlmutter, Donna Utke, Ann Wilhelmy, Pam Weeks, and the other women who donated money to support this project;

Carol Richards, for advice about funding;

Meda Chesney-Lind, University of Hawaii—Manoa, for computer consultation; and the faculty and staff at Antioch University—Seattle, for statistical and computer consultation;

Sharon Reed, for more personal consultation;

All the women who extended their hospitality to me while I was travelling doing interviews;

Sharon Stroble and Janyce Vick for coding questionnaires;

Philip Blumstein and Pepper Schwartz, University of Washington, for writing *American Couples*, from which I learned so much, and for the use of their questionnaire, from which my own was developed;

The Still-Life Coffeehouse, for keeping me going;

The Freemont Place Book Company, for being right next door;

Barbara Grier and Donna McBride, of Naiad Press, for liking the idea of this study when it was only an idea, and for seeing it through to its final form;

And my special thanks to the women who sent me questionnaires and granted me interviews. This is your story. It's a joy and an honor for me to tell it.

To Connie
Who is the reason for it all

TABLE OF CONTENTS

LIST OF TABLES

xiii

Chapter 4: Sexuality

Chapter 5: Problems

Chapter 6: Children, Family and Friends

Preface

When I became a lesbian thirty two years ago this Thanksgiving, I was overwhelmed by the presence of my new love: her look, her voice, her words, her body. I was, for the first time as a grownup, passionately joined to another person. I had fallen in love.

I was also eerily alone. I was faced with new feelings, behaviors, thoughts, and fantasies, but not yet a new identity; that was a long time coming. Nothing I was doing, or thinking of doing, or wanting to do had been laid out for me. I had to create it myself.

We women who love women, we lesbians, have all had this experience. Fortunately, the frenzy of first love gives us the power to create that first explosion of joining. We are not really alone; we have our sexual energy propelling us. (I've found a great word for the intensity of this first love: nympholepsy, a "frenzy that seizes one possessed by a demon," or a "frenzy of emotion, especially for an unattainable ideal.")

Remember what a chaotic guide this energy was? Where were other, more sober, wiser influences? Where were other women-who-loved-women to reassure and counsel us, to give us their wisdom and their blessing? This is the sense in which you and I were alone. We lacked experienced, wiser lesbians to guide us through these first explorations. We lacked role models.

My problems with the absence of guides didn't stop once I emerged from this first love experience. My first three lesbian relationships all lasted three years. I concluded that it is the nature of lesbian relationships to be intense, absorbing, difficult, and three years long. I was using my own experience to project a definition of what it is to be a lesbian.

I then fell in love with a woman who had been married to a man — who thus had marriage as a model — and that relationship, and my subsequent one, each lasted ten years. I concluded that lesbian relationships can, and probably do, break up after ten years or so.

Again, I was concluding something important about the nature of lesbianism based on a sample experience of one: my own. True, my own is the only experience I really care about, but it is not the stuff from which all lesbian experience can be generalized. Which is just as well.

For some reason . . . my age, my luck, my partner, dwindling energy, growing wisdom, the political climate, the goddess . . . I have committed myself to staying with my partner Connie "forever" (more about "forever" later). But how to do this? As usual I find myself without role models, this time for staying in a long-term lesbian couple.

I sought the only available role models, heterosexual ones, of course. I read a good book, *Married People. Staying Together in the Age of Divorce* (1985), where the author, Francine Klagsbrun, travelled around the country interviewing couples married fifteen years or more to find out to what they attributed their longevity. It occurred to me that I could do something similar for lesbians: Search out the women who have stayed together in loving couples for a long time, ask them about their relationships, how they have weathered their problems, why they didn't break up, how they do money, jobs and sex, what their joys and special pleasures have been, what advice they have for us.

This book reports what these women have told us.

* * * * *

I need to say something here about the word lesbian. Many of the women in my study do not like this word and do not use it to describe themselves. And, if my book has reached the diverse audience I hope it will, many of you now reading these words feel the same. The word lesbian for you may have connotations of radical, political, young, promiscuous.

You may prefer gay women, or women-who-love-women, or simply women. I believe that it is part of the diversity of our culture and our history that particular names mean significantly different things to the many different women among us. I respect those preferences and the realities they express.

It is also true, as my publisher has convinced me, that the women who are most likely to buy this book will most easily recognize and identify the term lesbian. I thus have used it in the title, and use it liberally throughout the book. I hope those of you for whom this is a difficult word can suspend your discomfort and, for the purposes of this book, take it as simply a generic denotation for women who love women. Thank you.

* * * * *

For those of you who like to study a map before you start a journey, read Chapter 1 next. For those who like a good story, let me begin by introducing you to one of the long-term couples. The names and other identifying characteristics of these women have, of course, been changed to preserve their privacy. But there is nothing here that I have made up. This is not a work of fiction. These women are real.

STORY 1:

PAT (age 74) & ANNA (age 73): 52 years together

Pat: We didn't agree on anything except sex for a long time.

Anna: Oh, that's right.

Pat: There was nothing we agreed on.

Anna: We didn't like the same authors, we didn't care for the same leisure pursuits, we weren't the same social class, any of those things.

Pat: I once got her a horse, just once. That was a disaster.

1

Anna: Well, it didn't hurt me. I wasn't exactly in control of that critter, but one can't have all those facets polished at that time of life!

Susan: So when you say you were similar about sex, do you mean you were monogamous, was that the similarity you mean?

Pat: No. . . .

Anna: We enjoyed each other.

Pat: We enjoyed each other sexually.

Pat and Anna live in a comfortable, rustic one-bedroom cabin that Pat built nearly thirty years ago. Their place has a ranch atmosphere, which reflects Pat's love of horses, though she hasn't owned a horse in more than fifty years. They're on a couple of acres on the outskirts of Santa Fe, in the middle of what has become a wealthy development. Houses worth half a million dollars are going up nearby, and the soaring annual property taxes will soon outstrip Pat's entire income for the year. They may have to move, losing their retirement home. They'll be rich in money, but poorer in spirit.

Although Pat dreads the day ("I had intended on being carried out of here feet first."), Anna is not devastated. Her arthritis makes it hard for her to get around the place, and besides, "I think it would be nice to live in a place that had white plastered walls or wallpaper . . . not luxury, mind you . . . some refinements."

This is a butch-femme couple.

Anna: There used to be a time back when we

first got together, when dykes were separated into butches and femmes. Pat still rather believes in that because that's the way she was brought up. And you see less and less of that, so that you can't detect anyone who is the autocratic head of the household.

Susan: At least not by looking you can't tell.

Anna: Talk to them for a bit and you know rather well. Yes. Even though it might not be the one who does the plumbing.

Pat dresses like a man. Everyone dresses with care for an interview, and Pat wore a Western shirt and tailored pants, a leather belt, leather vest, and string tie. She has short hair and walks with a cowboy's swagger. Anna doesn't really look like a femme, she dresses casually, but she seems more feminine compared to Pat.

Pat gets her way simply by stating what she wants; Anna uses more subtle tactics. When I asked what they thought had held them together all these years, Anna said: "I credit it to my sweet disposition."

Susan: Say more.

Anna: It does stabilize a marriage, you know.

Pat: Well, she's got a sweet disposition; I don't.

Susan: So somebody in a couple has to have a sweet . . .

Anna: Somebody needs one. You can write that down!

Another way they put it is that Anna doesn't care about things and Pat does. Pat cares about a lot of things and is a difficult sort of person; Anna doesn't care about so many things and is a good-natured sort of person. Anna: "We suit each other madly well: I cater to her and she takes care of me. I don't consider it an unequal relationship."

Anna has to be indirect to get her way. She talks about things with Pat for a long time before anything happens. In fact, she talks about whatever she wants so subtly Pat may not even know what they're talking about ("Little discussions that she didn't know we were having.") Pat says she knows when this is happening, when she's being manipulated. She probably does . . . at least some of the time.

Pat and Anna got together in Topeka, Kansas, fifty-two years ago, in the 1930s, when they were both in their early twenties. Pat: "I didn't know I was gay per se, but I knew I wasn't the same as a lot of other kids." By the time they met, Pat had already been in a gay relationship for seven years (since she was fourteen years old), but she said that was just "immature girlfriends." When that relationship ended, she was hurt, so she wasn't looking for anyone, but she knew that she wanted somebody she was going to stay with.

When she first knew Anna: "I would see her coming down the street, and my heart would just stop." Anna at the time was enjoying a two- or three-year free and promiscuous phase; she had a wonderful time being sexual with everybody, everybody female that is. Anna: "When I discovered the gay world, it was like opening a door that hadn't been opened before." Pat knew she wanted this girl,

4

but also knew she didn't want somebody who was going to be unfaithful; monogamy was terrifically important to her.

> *Anna:* Pat equates sex and love as the same thing, you see. You can have love without sex, but you can't have sex without love.
> *Susan:* Do you agree with that?'
> *Anna:* No doubt that's very admirable . . . Now you know! I think sex is sex.
> *Susan:* Is being monogamous hard for you?
> *Anna:* Yes, very difficult.
> *Susan:* Did you and Pat talk about it? Was it negotiable, or was it not?
> *Anna:* No, it was not negotiable.

Pat had a unique approach:

> *Anna:* After we had dated a couple of times — and this means, my dear, simply going somewhere for a drink and perhaps a chaste kiss at the end of the evening — she asked me to come out and stay with her, and I did, in this twin bed. But she didn't wish to have sex. She was the most hard to get of anyone I'd encountered at that time . . . hard to get sexually. It made her seem very special.
>
> Of course I couldn't go out and whore around while I was in this bed, because I was in the bed! So she put me on a sex-free diet for a period of what . . . how long was that, for heaven's sake?

Pat: About a month. I wanted her to prove that she really wanted to stay with me. That was my point . . that she wasn't going to be running around whoring all the time.

After a few weeks Pat was convinced of Anna's loyalty. They got together, and they've been together ever since.

The sexual part of their relationship was real important, especially to Anna, she thinks more important to her than it ever was to Pat. Many years ago Pat had a hysterectomy, and became completely uninterested in sex. ("You run out of steam.") She tried to get some help from doctors, but hormone treatments didn't help.

As a result, Pat and Anna stopped having sex in their relationship thirty years ago. This was hard for Anna who enjoys sex; it was hard for Pat, who felt Anna deserved a sexual relationship: "She was just in the prime of life, and there she was, cut off from sex." Now they take pleasure in sleeping together, which they've done all their lives, cuddling, being close. Pat: "It's still very nice to be in bed together."

I asked them what it is they like best about being in a long-term relationship. Pat: "You have no loose ends, and you feel comfortable, and you feel like somebody cares. It's kinda like a safety net. And you know, the older you get, the more you need somebody to shore you up."

Pat's an example of what I call the fierce woman, women who were fiercely committed right from the beginning. With the strength of their personality and

6

their unwavering commitment, these women made their relationships persist, sometimes despite the more hesitant commitment of their partners. Anna describes what she likes about a long-term relationship:

> *Anna:* I've grown accustomed to her face, to quote. We have relatively few surprises from each other anymore. So that makes for a far more equal living than to have to creep around and adjust for something you're not aware of. And, also, whether we suited each other initially, we sure do now . . . I think we rubbed the edges off each other."

Both women, in different ways, are saying that in a long-term relationship you don't have to be afraid anymore, of being lonely, of not measuring up, of surprises and the unknown.

I asked how close they had ever come to breaking up.

> *Pat:* Well, we've had rows and then we've thought about it a couple days later and we couldn't even remember what we were fighting about. But I think if you don't have rows once in awhile, one of you is really a Milquetoast.
>
> *Anna:* We used to say that if we were to separate, the one who wanted the separation had to give the other one fifty dollars. And we could never get fifty dollars

7

together . . . It was so impractical, really, to split up. Just too much of a nuisance.

Anna: And imagine, after fifty-two years, for Pete's sake . . . Where's my right arm? Who's gonna take the garbage out?

Pat: Who's gonna wash the car?

Anna: This is what romance is made of.

The biggest problem they have, the thing they fight about the most, is Anna's drinking.

Susan: Has alcohol ever been a problem for either of you or the relationship, or . . .

Anna: Oh, yes, with me essentially.

Susan: Did you stop drinking or do you drink moderately, or what . . .

Anna: Oh no. I drink some of each. Sometimes I'm moderate and sometimes I go overboard. And since gin's my tipple, that's a pretty rough way to go. Pat does get smashed every now and then, but sometimes she doesn't recognize it. And most of the time, she does drink in moderation.

Susan (later): I was one of those people, I could not have one drink. I couldn't do it.

Anna: Oh, I don't think I'd be interested in one drink.

Both of them drink unabashedly, and have from the beginning. Alcohol has been important to their relationship and to the culture they lived in most of their lives. Pat can moderate her drinking, but Anna gets out of control. Then they fight about how Anna

8

behaves, especially if she's in public. Pat would like her to be able to cut back, something she can't do.

Susan: How long has this fighting about Anna's drinking been going on?

Pat: Oh, about fifty-two years.

Susan: Some things never change, do they?

Pat: They never do.

Friends have always been important to Pat and Anna. They had hordes of friends in Southern California during the thirty-five years they lived there (Anna: "And by the way, it used to be a heavenly place."), once they left Kansas the first year they were together. In L.A. they had rowdy, fun parties all the time. Their best friends were two gay men who lived next door.

Anna: We used to have mad, mad parties between our place and theirs, and the neighbors accepted us up to a certain point because they thought we were whores. Then they discovered that we were gay ladies, and they yanked their kids home!

Their jobs were adventures too. Remember, this was the Great Depression, so Pat and Anna started with no money at all.

Pat: Back in Topeka we had a winter with thirty days that it never got up to zero. So we said, "We haven't got any money, we might as well go to California and have no money where it's warm."

9

They applied for relief so they could qualify for jobs with the W.P.A. Anna pounded nails in picture frames. (Pat: "She was about as mechanical as nothing, you know, pounded all her fingers. So I called up and quit for her one day.") They were ghostwriters:

> *Pat:* We had some really, really interesting people as our customers . . . We had a Russian refuge customer whose name was Nikolai Nikolski, and on cold, cold windy nights he would come over — he drove an old Rolls Royce — and he would bring a bottle of rum, and we would have rum tea, and he would read his poetry in Russian, which we could not understand one word, but it was beautiful.

World War II began, and Pat was hired as the first woman flight mechanic.

> *Pat:* I've always been mechanical. I learned to drive by driving a car, a race car, on a half-mile dirt track. I just like mechanical things. So they got me off of relief when I was on WPA, and first they sent me to a school to learn to rivet. Which is a damn boring job. I went from there to a place where they were modifying and overhauling cars to send from one theater of operations to another. I was working on Jeeps. I was doing brakes and things like that.
>   One day they came along and said,

"Everybody stop working and clean up because we're going to have a lot of big shots come along to inspect." And I said, "I'm not going to do it." And the boss said, "Why?" And I said, "Because what the soldiers need is these jeeps; they don't need generals to come and see if we've swept the floor!" And he said, "You can't do that." And I said, "The hell I can't; I'm not under you. I'm a civilian."

And so by God they made me in charge of the parts warehouse to keep the thing going, and the mechanic and the captain brought me around a bottle of scotch and said, "We've been wantin' to tell him that for a long time."

Pat and Anna say their young friends aren't as interested in how they've managed to stay together as they are in hearing their stories about what it's been like to be gay the past fifty years. Their friends show good judgment. These women have been out their entire lives together; their story is the history of openly gay women during those years. They are our past, in its most free, least constrained form.

Now Pat and Anna have retired to Santa Fe, where they again have a good group of friends, six to eight long-term couples. It's important to these couples that each couple in their group has been together a long time. In fact, one of the women said she was pretty sure she and her partner couldn't have gotten into that group of women if they hadn't been together more than ten years.

11

Why do Pat and Anna think they've stayed together?

Pat: I think it's because we made up our minds we wanted to stay together. We would rather stay together than not stay together, and I really think that's the basis . . . we consider ourselves as one person, really.

Anna: That's right.

Chapter 1
Beginnings

I should tell you before we get too far into this that I don't have an answer for the question, How do long-term lesbian couples stay together? What's THE secret for a lasting relationship?

The women in this book tell me they don't have a secret. Why they've stayed together is a mystery to them too. "It feels to me almost as if it's an accident, or just luck and/or fate. We didn't plan to stay together — time just passed and we still were!" (Jane, age 52, a 31-year couple)

Do not despair and close this book prematurely in disappointment. These women do have things to say to all of us that we need to know.

They tell us the most important single thing that we need to know; that they have indeed stayed together.

They tell us how they got together and how things have changed for them over the years.

They talk about their troubles — a lot of them serious troubles — and how they got through them.

They talk about sex, money, children, and health, about fighting and making up, about how they almost broke up but didn't.

They offer advice.

They recount their joys and pleasures.

Through it all they talk of love, of falling in love, of learning to love more deeply, of finding ways to reclaim and rebuild love, of sustaining love over years.

These women have a lot to say, powerful things, scary things, true things, inspiring things. They all say they don't have THE answer. But they have some awfully good ideas.

Purpose of the Study

I have written this book so that you will know that lesbians create and enjoy long-term couple relationships. That's my primary purpose and the single most important thing this book can accomplish. Just to give these women a chance to say: Yes, we're out here; yes, we're happy. And, by implication: Yes, if you want to, you can stay together too.

This sounds like a simple purpose. But remember who we lesbians are, and how radical are the simplest things we do. The fact that we love women is our most radical act. Loyal members of our misogynist society hate women. As lesbians we know and live a subversive truth, that women create happiness and satisfaction for each other independent of men. Our society regards this as an outrage. The existence of lesbian couples — many even with children — demonstrates that women create stable, productive, supportive families without a thought to men and their needs. This fact challenges a fundamental doctrine of our society, that women exist to serve men. Lesbian existence is thus sacrilege.

Is it any surprise, then, that lesbians are hidden, that lesbian couples are invisible? Adrienne Rich, in her 1980 article, "Compulsory Heterosexuality and Lesbian Existence," (*Signs*, Vol. 5, No. 4) identifies "the Great Silence . . . in history and culture" that surrounds "women and particularly lesbian existence." We lesbians and the larger society suffer because of this great silence.

Our society suffers because the alternatives that lesbian existence and lesbian creativity offer are unavailable to everyone, particularly to women who would most obviously benefit from knowing what we know and doing some of the things we are able to do. I think of Mattie, a black lesbian, who told me what was to her, and to me, a surprising thing:

"My boss, a heterosexual woman, said to me that when she looks to change her

15

relationship, to improve it, she looks to the lesbians in her life. Because, she says, heterosexuals have no role models for positive, equal relationships. I was just absolutely blown away." (Mattie, age 33, 12-year couple)

We lesbians are always bemoaning the fact that we don't *have* role models. But it had never occurred to me that we *are* role models for those people lucky enough to know us. The more people who know about the successful experiments we lesbians conduct daily in fashioning our non-traditional lives, the more people would be challenged to try their own hands at constructing creative social forms . . . and the less rigid and oppressive our lives would be . . . and the more powerful women would be . . . and the more humane and liveable our society would be . . . and so on.

The silence that surrounds what we lesbians do hurts us more directly than anyone else. This silence means we have little idea of what lesbians are doing, thinking, feeling, creating, and achieving outside of our own moment in history and our own small group (of whatever age, race, social class, nationality, etc. we and our friends happen to be). Thus we can easily underestimate our own diversity, vitality, and power. The many choices we have are hidden from us. We can wind up living our "non-traditional" lives in rigid conformity to small enclaves within our own subculture.

Take long-term lesbian relationships. Some of us know almost exclusively only lesbians who — like ourselves — are in long-term couples. We have little patience with and no knowledge of young, single lesbians. In fact, we don't even like the word lesbian all that much.

Some of us know only lesbians who — like ourselves — are single, dating, and committed to the exploration of multiple relationships. We have little respect for and no knowledge of older, coupled lesbians. We like the word lesbian, maybe even with add-ons, like lesbian feminist, or radical lesbian.

Then there's what I suspect is a huge group of us who are in between: We know only other lesbians who — like ourselves — are coupled, committed and semi-monogamous for three, four, five years, but who then break up and are single for a while (even if it's only a very short while) between relationships. We envy and emulate both ends of the spectrum, the secure coupled women when we're coupled; the free singles when we're single. Or is it that we envy the singles when we're coupled, and the couples when we're single? Well, whatever, we know only a little bit about either group. We're fine with the word lesbian, just not too loud, please.

Of the groups I've described, I think we know least about the long-term couples. Many of us have no firsthand knowledge of long-term couples we know are lesbian. We may suspect certain women of being lesbians, but we don't know and feel we cannot ask. These couples are often very closeted, sometimes afraid of exposure even to other lesbians.

"I am a private person, and seldom feel the need to share my sexual preference with those who are not considered close friends. I am not ashamed, I'm just not open, at all, with strangers." (Victoria, age 70, a 31-year couple)

17

"My own experience shows lesbian relationships can last, and I believe there are thousands of other couples hiding in big cities and mountains who have been together a long time, but we don't see them! Nobody saw us our first nineteen years or more due to the closet." (Jane, age 52, a 31-year couple)

It is not surprising that many of us have meager knowledge of such couples. And what we don't know about isn't available to us as a pattern to emulate. We can't use long-term lesbian couples as role models if we don't know any. Nor does it help if we suspect we know such couples, but feel we can't get close to them because of their ingrained reticence or our respectful timidity. Thus the "great silence" works to separate us from those whose experience we need and want.

The experience of a long-term relationship, the experience of "forever" is something many of us say we want. But let me make an important disclaimer here. This book does not argue, and should not be taken to mean, that permanent coupleness is a form morally superior to other ways lesbians can relate. There are lots of good things to be said for multiple simultaneous relationships, serial relationships, and no relationships (though in this era of AIDS, special care must be taken by those who choose multiple and serial relationships). I may be interested in coupling and in permanence for myself. Many of you who have picked up this book are presumably interested for yourselves. But not all of us are interested. Each woman must make the arrangements for intimacy that suit her best. Coupling may not be for you right now. Or ever, for that matter. I'm not saying it should be. Nor would the long-term couples; they know too much about the realities of coupling to wish longevity on anyone who doesn't want it. Victoria (age 70 and thirty-one years in her couple) cautions,

". . . building a life together means weighing carefully the pluses of making plans for the future and collecting memories to share against the minuses of having to make the daily adjustments and compromises that any two people face."

Others express this balancing differently, but the point here is that, as we know, nothing worth achieving comes without cost. No enterprise is without its drawbacks, its terrors, its losses. Being part of a couple has its full share. It's not for sissies. All this having been said, I know (I fear?) many of us persist in wanting a relationship that lasts. A 1978 study (reported in Bell and Weinberg, *Homosexualities: A Study of Diversity among Men and Women*, 1978) documents what we know already from our own lives, that lesbians attach great importance to permanent relationships. Sixty percent of the "women-identified-women" who were part of this large research project said a permanent relationship is either "very important" (25 percent) or "the most important thing in life" (35 percent).

If we needed any more evidence, our behavior when we couple implies a desire for permanence. We become monogamous. We move in together. We say things about forever, and we are devastated when the

19

relationship ends. We want to stay together. We intend to stay together. But we don't.

Lesbians are not, of course, the only people in our society who break up. A recent book based on the 1980 census, *American Families and Households* (1987), reports that the chance that a heterosexual marriage will end in divorce has been rising steadily in virtually all Western countries and is now close to fifty percent in the United States.

The book *American Couples* (1983) by sociologists Philip Blumstein and Pepper Schwartz has important information about non-traditional couples. This unique large-scale study compared 4,314 heterosexual couples (married and co-habiting), 1,875 gay male couples, and 1,723 lesbian couples on a large number of variables organized around the themes of money, work, and sex. What is relevant here is the break-up rate for each type of couple. The researchers followed up a sample of their couples eighteen months after the initial surveys, and found that 48 percent of the lesbian couples had broken up. This should be compared to 14 percent of the married couples, 29 percent of heterosexual co-habiting couples, and 36 percent of gay male couples. The researchers were astonished to find that more lesbian couples had broken up than any other type of couple, including gay males.

I know this finding violates a most cherished belief, that we women are more stable than those men. I can conjure up ways to explain away the data, the best being that lesbians who volunteer for such a study are an unstable lot to begin with, but the finding is nonetheless unsettling. Are the gay men who volunteered a more stable lot?

Let me summarize. It seems to me that many of us want to create permanent couple relationships for ourselves, that we have a great deal of trouble doing so, and that we have few if any guides to help us with our dilemma. A purpose of this book is to give us those guides. I hope they will help us match our hopes and our intentions with some realistic knowledge about what long-term is about.

Getting together is about romance. Staying together is about reality. The women who've talked with me want to tell you and me about the reality part . . . as well as the romance.

Design of the Study

This is the only large, nation-wide study of long-term lesbian couples that has been done. Other studies of lesbian couples suffer from a number of limitations. Some are either very small or very localized or both. Some are not really studies but observations based on a therapist's experiences with clients. Some do not focus on long-term couples. I want to describe in some detail the methodology of this study, because how one does a study affects the findings.

Finding the women I would talk with and send my questionnaires to was of major methodological significance, and a major challenge. Most studies of lesbians rely on the women's center in the city where the researcher's university is based to contact lesbians who want to participate. The researcher also asks in her/his sociology and psychology classes for volunteers. (You know the joke: Everything we know about

21

human behavior is based on the reported behavior of male college sophomores? Would it were just a joke!) This method of recruiting "subjects" results in repeated studies of the same types of lesbians: relatively young, relatively well educated, fairly uncloseted. These lesbians also seem to be relatively unattached.

I felt I had to go about finding my lesbians differently. So, I did what we all do when we need help: I asked my friends . . . who asked their friends . . . who asked their friends. (The technical term for this method is "snowball sampling," which I might have chosen to do for its name alone.) Over a period of eighteen months (March, 1988 to August, 1989) I was put in touch with a large number of long-term couples, the majority of whom were unknown to me personally.

Using the snowball method I was able to find many women who would be unlikely to participate in most lesbian studies because they would never know about them. Thirty-five percent of the women in this study are neither active in the lesbian/gay community nor subscribers to lesbian or gay periodicals. Researchers using standard methods to contact subjects would never uncover these women.

This method also seems appropriate to the subject of long-term couples. Logically, many long-term couples will be made up of older women, women who are less likely to be found hanging out around college women's centers waiting to volunteer for sociology studies. I have thus found women we rarely hear from, lesbians who don't get to tell their stories except to their own friends.

These are some good things about the sample: It

is large, it is geographically diverse, it is made up of older, more closeted women. But there's one thing it's not: it isn't random. No study of a stigmatized population will be able to meet science's requirement of a random sample, precisely because the population under study is hidden and thus cannot form a base from which the sample can be randomly drawn.

This means that what we find out from the women who participated in my study cannot be generalized. We cannot draw conclusions about all long-term lesbian couples from information about these few — even if quite a few — long-term lesbian couples.

If you're willing, then, to accept that what is true for these women may or may not be true for others, we can proceed. This doesn't mean that how they've lived and what they say isn't important, touching and wise. It is. It's true for them, and — after all — it's their story we're telling. And their story we need to hear.

* * * * *

One hundred eight couples (216 women) participated in the study. Each woman in the couple filled out a questionnaire, independent of her partner. There were twenty-four pages of questions, some where the women could check a particular response, many where she could express herself at length.

I interviewed 34 of the 108 couples. In choosing who to interview I gave preference to couples who had been together a longer time. I also made sure I interviewed couples who represented something that was true of some important segment of the sample as

23

a whole, e.g., they were women of color, or they had children, or they were both Jewish, or there was a significant age difference, or they were each other's first relationship.

Each interview took from three to five hours and was almost always done in the couple's home, usually around the kitchen or dining room table where all women seem to feel comfortable. I interviewed both partners together. The interview consisted of: (1) conversation that followed up things the women had said in their questionnaires; (2) other questions that would be difficult to answer in writing; (3) whatever came up that we three wanted to talk about.

Any study necessarily omits some things, either through lack of space or time, oversight, or the simple need to limit the scope of the project. Let me discuss some of those things here.

I did not include a category for self-employment when I asked the women about jobs. As a result, the number of self-employed respondents is certainly underestimated. I think lesbians often choose some form of self-employment — it makes us less vulnerable to job discrimination — and lesbian studies should design their methodology to take this into account.

I did not question the women about their use of alcohol or drugs, even though alcohol and drug abuse is a documented problem among lesbians. Doing so in any depth would have added several pages to an already long questionnaire, but with hindsight I wish I had done so anyway. Sometimes the women volunteered important information about their use (see the chapter on Problems), but without having asked, I cannot conclude anything about the pattern

24

of alcohol or drug use within the group as a whole. This is clearly an area where significant research remains to be done.

After the fact I am also aware of the importance of psychotherapy to many individuals and couples; the amount of time some of the couples have spent taking care of relatives other than children; the central place pets play in some relationships; and of a history of physical abuse in some couples. None of these issues can be dealt with systematically because questions about them did not appear in the questionnaire. I do discuss each topic when the material offered makes it possible.

Criteria for Selecting the Sample:
What is a Long-Term Lesbian Couple?

A researcher always has to decide who it is she wants to study; she has to establish criteria for selecting her sample: Which is another way of asking: Who is this book about? I used three criteria for choosing the women in this book:

1. The women considered themselves a couple;
2. They had been a couple for ten years or more;
3. They were sexual with each other at some time in their relationship.

The first criterion created no problem. Each of these relationships was defined as a couple relationship by the women themselves, though what each woman means by "couple" may vary greatly.

The second criterion, the choice of ten years or

more to define "long-term," was arbitrary, based on my desire that these couples have lasted longer than my own two long relationships. Also in my mind was the psychologist Carl Whitaker's belief that it takes (heterosexual) couples ten years to abandon their illusions about each other, ten years to see each other as the people they really are.

Applying this second criterion was only a problem when couples broke up for some period during the course of the relationship. I counted the length of the relationship to be from its beginning until the present. I did not deduct time spent apart. So, if the relationship began twelve years ago, and the couple split up for one year, this study would credit it with a twelve-year relationship.

The third criterion created huge problems, at least for me. If I want to study long-term lesbian couples, who am I going to consider lesbian?

This is not a problem of the word lesbian, though I had to be careful about the word too. Had I insisted on "the L word," many women whose experiences we need to know about would have eliminated themselves from the study. In fact, not everyone wants to call themselves gay either:

> "We identify simply as two women living together in a primary relationship." (Agnes, age 75, 41-year couple)

A woman in a twelve-year couple sums up the problem we all have in choosing the right name:

> "We are best friends and lovers. I still haven't found the right descriptive term, really.

Maybe because I'm arrogant to think we're unique (I know *every* relationship is.)

Partner sounds like a law firm. Wife sounds like June Cleaver. Lesbian lover still carries a bit of the National Enquirer to many people, doesn't it? It's still not a neutral term. Gay seems to be for men, mostly.

I'm still looking for the right phrase. I don't know if it's been invented yet." (Carrie, age 35)

What I did about the problem of which term to use was the following: I described the study in my materials used to solicit participants as "a study of intimate relationship between women" and used the word women throughout. The questionnaires used the word lesbian, sometimes lesbian/gay. In the interviews I used the word women until the couple themselves gave me a clue as to their preferred word and their comfort level with other words. Often we discussed explicitly the connotations different words had for them.

But the third criterion problem — who is a lesbian — is not about the name. It's about intention and experience and behavior. What do we mean when we say we're women who love women? Mothers and daughters love each other. Sisters love each other. Friends love each other. What is different about our love for each other? Why aren't we just friends?

The answer is that lesbians (or partners, or wives, or lovers, or gays, or two women living together) — in addition to loving each other's minds and hearts and souls — we love each other's bodies; we're sexual together. It's the sexual nature of our relationships

27

that defines us, that makes us more than friends. I don't mean to say that we're only sexual beings or that we're always sexual beings or even that we're most importantly sexual beings. But I do believe it is because we are all attracted to women sexually that we share a history and a culture. It is this bond that ties us to our partners and ties us to each other. It is this truth about ourselves that makes us who we are and has made us choose the kinds of lives we are living.

I didn't get clear for myself about all this until I met Leila and Margery. Leila and Margery are 93-years-old and have been together sixty-five years. They live together in a room with twin beds and bath in a Catholic nursing home in Milwaukee, Wisconsin, where I found them one summer Sunday. I had been told about them by a friend of a friend who had worked in the nursing home a year earlier and remembered this couple. They were a bit surprised to see this stranger who wanted to talk, but thankful for the company. Leila was happy to talk; Margery was happy to sit alongside and doze.

So, surrounded by the mementoes they'd kept, Leila told me about their long lives together. She'd moved in with Margery and her mother in 1924. Her own mother had died two years later, and her father remarried, so she didn't need to go home to Minnesota to take care of him. Leila and Margery had both worked for the railroad. They shared their money and at one point spent all of it taking care of Margery's mother when she got sick. They bought a summer cabin in northern Wisconsin and moved there when they retired. She talked about how much they enjoyed their many friends; how important the

Catholic Church was to them both; how they moved into the nursing home five years ago; and how Margery then gave up the car she'd driven all her life and from that point on began to deteriorate mentally. Leila said, ". . . so she parted with the car. And that parted with her life." Margery wakes up: "My life went out with the car."

They divided up tasks: Leila: "I cooked, she done everything else." And they still do: Leila: "My memory is good, but her walking is much better." Margery: "We each have something."

They never had a fight: "We had no problems." But now Leila worries because she gets short-tempered and impatient with Margery, who has difficulty remembering.

> *Leila:* We've had such a wonderful life together that you wouldn't want to break it. (in tears)
> *Susan:* You must love each other very much.
> *Leila:* Yeah, we do. She's been so good to me, all my life. That I couldn't help but love her for all the years, the kindness. It's remarkable. . . . I'm having a little crying spell, Margery. Do you care?
> *Margery:* And I'm just having a little snooze.

Leila and Margery built a long and happy life together. They love each other deeply. But they are not lesbians, not by my definition. I asked Leila,

> *Susan:* There is one thing I want to ask . . . Some women who are together now are sexual with each other. You know, they

hug and kiss and are sexual. Were you ever that with each other?"

Leila: Oh, no. No, no. No, this is not . . . no part of the friendship whatever. Because we have been friends, and good friends, and that's what it's been all of our lives. Because to me this other, this is especially for the male and female. And this is our life, and this is the way we should live. And we believe in living up to the rules and regulations of our bringing-up. And so this is the way we judge our lives, and this is the way we want to stay.

Margery (who woke up for this): . . . never had any difficulty. . . .

Leila: No reason why we would . . . when you don't have . . . don't have desires for . . . I think that's what's wrong with the whole world today. There's too much sex. And we . . . there was never any sex brought up when we were young. We never heard it during our lifetime. When I think of what goes on today, I can't believe it.

I believe Leila and Margery, that the mores of their time in history and the doctrines of their Church meant they never even considered a sexual relationship.

The fact that they weren't sexual has other implications for their relationship beyond the physical experience they did not share. They never fell in love. Leila describes her moving in with Margery as a matter of convenience; there's no excitement about it, no charge. Their subsequent decisions to stay together are interpreted as practical choices, not as assumptions of a committed couple. Since they were doing nothing they had to hide, they never experienced any guilt or shame or internalized homophobia about their relationship. Two women living together was perfectly acceptable to their society as long as their parents were not being neglected. Nor did they suffer any discrimination. Not being lesbians, they would be immune to the perils of being openly deviant.

All of this meant Leila and Margery didn't really see themselves as a couple. This is the only interview I did where it was difficult to get the women to talk about "us" instead of about "me." Leila wanted to tell me about *her* life; she had trouble thinking in terms of *their* life.

We often hear the sexual part of our relationships belittled, by others and by ourselves: What I do in bed is such a small part of my life; We're just like everybody else except for our sexual preference; Why is everyone so excited about a little thing like sex when there are so many other more important things about us?

I believe that our sexual lives are the foundation of our lives with women. Without our sexual attraction for women we would be like Leila and Margery, lifelong devoted friends, but at what cost: We would never have fallen in love, never lusted after each other, never felt sick with anxiety and desire. We would never know how powerfully passion bonds nor how wrenching is loss. We would not know the terrors of being different. We would not fear exposure, nor be devastated by rejection. We would not have to deal with self-hatred. We would not have comrades in battle.

We would be innocent. We would not be lesbians.

It is our sexuality that sets the stage for the whole story.

Description of the Sample

The 216 women live in 21 different states of the United States. Thirty-five percent are from the Pacific Northwest, 17 percent are Midwesterners, 15 percent are from California, and 11 percent from the Southwest. The other regions — the East/Southeast, Texas, Alaska, and Hawaii — together contributed the remaining 22 percent.

While there is a good distribution of longevity among the 108 couples who participated, it was much easier to find lesbian couples who had been together ten to fourteen years than it was to find couples who had been together longer. Nonetheless, 24 percent of the couples have been together twenty years or more. Table 1.1 gives the breakdown of longevity.

This study is unique in giving many older lesbians a chance to tell us about their lives. Nearly one-third of the group (seventy women) are 51 years old or older. Ten women are 71 or older. Table 1.2 shows the age distribution.

On the whole these lesbians are highly educated, far more so than women in the general population. (In 1987, only 16.5 percent of women age 25 or older had a college degree or more. *Statistical Abstracts of the United States,* 1989.) Eighty percent of the

TABLE 1.1 LONGEVITY OF THE COUPLES

Number of years together	Number of couples	Percent of couples
10 to 14 years	56	51.9
15–19 years	25	23.1
20–24 years	13	12.0
25–29 years	6	5.6
30–34 years	4	3.7
35 or more years	4	3.7
Total	108	100.0

lesbians in this group have at least a college degree, and nearly half have a post-college degree.

Fortunately for diversity, twelve women in this study are high school graduates or less, so we hear from a few women who have devoted less of their lives to school. Table 1.3 shows the distribution of educational attainment.

The lesbians in the sample overwhelmingly work

TABLE 1.2 AGE OF THE WOMEN

Age	Number of women	Percent of women
Under 35 years	24	11.1
36–40 years	55	25.5
41–50 years	67	31.0
51–60 years	37	17.1
61–70 years	23	10.6
71 years or older	10	4.7
Total	216	100.0

TABLE 1.3 EDUCATION OF THE WOMEN

Education	Number of women	Percent of women
Less than high school graduation	3	1.4
High school graduate	9	4.2
Some college or post high school technical	31	14.4
College graduate	24	11.1
Some post college, academic or technical	46	21.3
Post college degree	103	47.6
Total	216	100.0

or have worked in the past. Only two women of the 216 classified themselves as full-time homemakers. Most work full-time for someone else (56.7 percent) or for themselves (9.8 percent), and 15.8 percent are now retired, but did work in the past. (For comparison, in 1988, 56 percent of all women age 16 or older worked outside the home. *Statistical Abstracts of the United States,* 1989.) Table 1.4 reports these data. (Whenever a total does not sum to 216 women, or 108 couples, it means some of the women did not respond to the question.)

The unusual amount of education of these women plus the fact that they all work or have done so is reflected in their incomes which, while not exorbitantly high are, on the whole, comfortable. Twenty percent earn $40,000 or more a year, and another 21 percent earn between $30,000 and $40,000 per year. Not everyone is moderately affluent, however. Nineteen women (8 percent) earn less than

TABLE 1.4 EMPLOYMENT STATUS

Employment status	Number of women	Percent of women
Full-time employed	122	56.7
Part-time	28	13.0
Unemployed, laid off, sick	5	2.3
Retired	34	15.8
Homemakers	2	0.9
Self-employed	21	9.8
Students	3	1.4
Total	215*	100.0

*Number of women who responded to this question.

$10,000 per year, which, unless they are paired with a richer partner, would leave them quite poor. Table 1.5 shows income.

A wide range of occupations were reported by the women. (These are the true occupations. I only

TABLE 1.5 INCOME

Income	Number of women	Percent of women
No reported income	2	0.9
Less than $4,999 per year	4	1.9
$5,000 to $9,999	13	6.1
$10,000 to $19,999	51	23.7
$20,000 to $29,999	56	26.0
$30,000 to $39,999	47	21.9
$40,000 to $49,999	18	8.4
$50,000 or more	24	11.2
Total	215*	100.0

*Number of women who responded to this question.

disguise material for purposes of confidentiality when I'm discussing individual women.) There are, however, twice as many teachers as any other occupation. Forty-two women teach at some level, twenty-four of them in colleges or universities.

The next three occupations are about equally represented: twenty-two therapists; twenty-one nurses and other medical support folk; and nineteen administrators, in business, government, or elsewhere. There are eleven social workers, nine accountants, three physicians, three attorneys, and three librarians. At least ten women own their own businesses, which include a kennel, a bakery, a day-care center, and an inn. Five women have something to do with publishing. There are three musicians, two writers, and four artists. There are also six secretaries, a groundskeeper and a dishwasher. Three women are engineers and four are in high level sales jobs. Plus there's a land surveyor, a TV editor, a chef, a newspaper reporter, three carpenters/contractors, a retired police sergeant, and a forester. Two women are unemployed and five are students.

The women who participated are overwhelmingly white. I only found six women of color, all of whom are paired with white women. Thus, of the 108 couples, 6 are interracial.

Although I made concerted efforts to find women of color, the fact that I was unable to do so is evidence of how partitioned our lesbian culture is, a reflection of the racial divisions of the larger society. Of course long-term couples exist among lesbians of color. The fact that I could not find more of them is a measure of how I, like the rest of us, am isolated within particular subgroups and find it difficult, in this case impossible, to create the contacts that would allow me to move into a different subgroup of our larger lesbian society.

This means that the study of long-term relationships among lesbians of color will need to be done by someone who is herself a lesbian of color and thus has the contacts to begin finding those couples. Although I think this is all right, since we all can speak most profoundly about what we know, I am still saddened not to include more racial diversity in this study.

There is more diversity of religious background. While more than half the women (56 percent) were raised Protestant, 25 percent were raised Catholic and 8.8 percent Jewish. Eight women were raised in some other religious tradition (e.g., Native American, Buddhist), and thirteen women report no particular religious training as children.

Plan of the Book

Each chapter is preceded by an in-depth look at one couple, like the presentation of Pat and Anna that preceded this chapter. Thus we meet a particular long-term couple in enough detail to get a feel for the unique character of their relationship. The couple segment is followed by a chapter that focuses on a theme that has emerged as important for all couples. The themes are: Commitment; Sameness/Difference; Sexuality; Problems; Children, Family and Friends; and Change and Conclusions.

There are two more things I need to say before we get into the meat (the tofu?) of the material.

Remember the discussion about methodology cautioned not to generalize from what these women have experienced to all long-term lesbian couples. There's a related caution that both the rules of methodology and the wisdom of living make necessary.

Just as you cannot generalize from these couples to others not studied, neither can you generalize from these couples to yourself or your couple. What is true for these women may or may not be a good idea for you. It is up to you to judge, to take what seems valuable and to discard what seems silly or painful or simply inappropriate. These women are authorities, but they are authorities only about their own unique relationship.

Pat says, "I don't know if you can advise people. I think everybody has to work it out their own way." Remember that.

Finally you may want this book to tell you what a "good" relationship is. Just as Pat can't give you advice, neither can I tell you how you and your partner should be or what the perfect lesbian couple should do. I'll tell you stories, pass on ideas and strategies, tell you about things that have worked for these women and things that haven't, things that satisfy them and other things that drive them crazy, about experiences they wish would never end, and others they hope will never repeat themselves. But no story, idea, strategy or experience is the "right" one. This is a book, not about what should be, but about what is.

STORY 2:

MARTHA (age 66) & DOTTY (age 67): 18 years together

Some women lead two complete lives, first as heterosexuals, then as lesbians. This is the story of one such couple, a story distinctive because of what these women had to do to come together. We all have to struggle to express our lesbian selves, but for these women . . . well, just read on.

Martha and Dotty met in a Presbyterian church in Iowa City twenty-three years ago. Dotty was the organist, Martha the minister's wife. Martha had three children, Dotty five. Each was happily married, in the conventional heterosexual sense of happy, and had been for many years. In fact they were conventional in every way: devoted mothers, loyal wives, active in their church. Then, astonishingly, they fell in love.

> *Dotty:* The first couple of years that we knew each other through church work, we didn't have too much intimate contact because a minister's wife is supposed to be friends with all the women in the congregation and not single anybody out, and I was very much aware of that.
>
> Martha was teaching music in a high school in Iowa City. One day she asked me to accompany a chorus that was going to perform, so we got a little bit more closely acquainted that way.
>
> *Martha:* Then I got sick and you brought flowers, and I thought that was awful nice of a parishioner to bring me flowers.
>
> *Dotty:* At that point I wasn't especially interested or anything, but then we went to a conference together in Des Moines, and on the way over we started talking about ourselves. . . .
>
> *Martha:* And theology, remember?
>
> *Dotty:* And theology, yes.
>
> *Martha:* She was very liberal and so was I.
>
> *Dotty:* When we got to the conference (she chuckles remembering) we had a rapport going to the point where we weren't very

40

pious. When we were having communion we started to giggle and could hardly behave ourselves . . . we just felt silly and happy.

Martha: I had associated with women all my life, and church women by the scores, but most of them talked about their babies and changing diapers and food and things like that.

Dotty talked a lot about brcoks and reading and theology, things that really were interesting to me. That was part of the rapport, I think . . . you kind of sense when the other person is interested in you.

So we were acting like little nuts, weren't we? And we were giggling and doin' all that kind of stuff.

Susan: How old were you at this point?

Dotty: I was 47 and Martha was 46. Old enough to know better!

I was talking with Martha and Dotty nearly twenty-five years after these events, sitting in the dining alcove of their tiny, neatly kept cement block house, in a small community not all that far from the original scene of the story they were telling. They still look much like the conventional church ladies they once were, dressed for the occasion of the interview in slacks and designer sweatshirts.

Every couple was nervous at first, wondering what I would be like (a cold detached scientist-type? an intrusive pest?). And I too was anxious (would they talk to me at all? would I be able to understand and appreciate them, no matter how different they were from me?). So I always started the interviews asking

41

the women how they got together. Each couple had such a thrilling story, one that is mostly so much fun to remember, that we would get past our worries in the shared excitement of their recounting how they fell in love.

At this early point in their emerging friendship, Martha and Dotty discovered that Martha was going to have to move with her husband to a new parish in Illinois.

Dotty: When we realized that she was going to have to go there, that we were going to be separated, things suddenly came to a head. We started passing notes back and forth to each other, and books, and poems, and. . . .

Susan: Did you have a feeling of being in love?

Dotty: Yeah, you could call it that. But we hadn't had any physical contact.

So just about Christmas time — her husband was in Des Moines that night — the choir was at her house. She asked me to go over a little bit early. She had the candles lighted and my favorite Christmas music on the record player, and we had a few minutes before the rest of the choir came. Just to visit, that's all at that point.

Then after choir practice, I was the last to leave. It was snowing heavily that night, and as I started to go out the door I stopped and turned back and she came toward me — she'd already said good-bye — and . . . I don't know . . . we just met in the middle in a clinch, and that was it.

Martha It was like magnets, you know?

Dotty: So we just held each other for, we don't know, maybe fifteen minutes or so.

Martha: Then I backed off and I said, "Wow. What is this?" And she said, "Oh, it's just the way you love your sister." And I said, "I never loved my sister this way."

Dotty: Well, I didn't either. My sister and I didn't get along most of the time. But it was something to say! I didn't know how else to explain it.

Martha: I think that was the point that we knew. From then on it was just a tearing feeling that we were gonna have to part.

Dotty: We assumed, each of us I'm sure, that we'd never hear from each other again. We didn't anticipate continuing this.

Martha: And remember, I gave you a going-away present of those special earrings from China.

Dotty: And I gave you an Ojibway symbol of eternal life.

Martha: And you cleaned out my oven.

Dotty: After I'd cleaned the oven, and had been there in that empty house for the hours it took me to clean the oven, I went home and went to bed for two days!

Once Martha moved away with her family, Dotty and Martha assumed their relationship was over, but it was just beginning. They simply couldn't let go of each other. They each kept a pad of paper close at hand and wrote to each other two or three times a day. Then every couple of days they'd mail the letter.

Martha had to rent a post office box to get hers without her husband intercepting them. She was teaching by now: "I would rush out of the classroom and go over to the public telephone and call her. We had a definite time once a week when she would be at the phone and I would call her."

The following summer they managed a five-day trip together, to the East Coast, where they visited cathedrals and churches. They rented a motel, with a double bed, and when they returned one night Dotty suggested Martha get drunk so she could have some firsthand experience for her counseling of alcoholics. (You know how these scenarios go, no justification is too ridiculous.)

> *Martha:* I put a few moves on you, you remember? I did something and you said . . .
>
> *Dotty:* I said, "Well, there are limits!"
>
> *Martha:* And I thought, hmmm, that's interesting, there are limits. So we got up the next day and dressed and were on the road when, all of a sudden she said, "You know, I was just thinkin' about last night . . . there are no limits."
>
> *Dotty:* So then we had a motel in New Haven, and that was the first night we really made love.
>
> *Martha:* We tried experimenting around, we didn't have the slightest idea what to do, you know?
>
> *Dotty:* Who all is listening to this? (Laughter)
>
> *Martha:* Okay, so New Haven, that was the

first time, on that trip. Then we tried to think of how we were going to be together. Because we knew from that point that we had to be together sometime or another. But we both agreed early on that she had these kids, and she would have to stay with them until her youngest was through high school. So that meant many, many years.
Dotty: It was ten years.

During those years there were many crises, times of ambivalence and failing nerve, and times of recommitment. Early on, Dotty, whose energies had been taken up raising her family, got a job. Martha was already teaching. Martha: "I said to her, if we're gonna get together eventually, we're gonna have to work. You better start exploring some way that you can work." Dotty got a job at a day-care center, and both women worked from then until their recent retirement.

Early in this period, Martha's relationship with her husband became more tense. Martha tried to break off the relationship: "Because my kids were puttin' on pressure and saying, you know, 'You're gonna break up the family.' " Martha and Dotty left at the end of one of their weekend getaways, vowing never to see each other again:

Dotty: But then a couple of days later, here came her regular letter.
Martha: There was no way. At that point I knew that it could not be called off. I tried. And couldn't do it. Just couldn't do it.

The following spring — two years after they'd fallen in love — they had a commitment ceremony.

Martha: We arranged to have a little commitment service in a chapel, beautiful little place. It had banks of flowers, and it was cherry blossom season. We went in the little church and said a few vows to each other."

Susan: What did you vow to each other?

Martha: It wasn't "I will stay with you forever" because we couldn't do that yet. We didn't know if we would ever be able to pull that off, because that meant breaking up her family and mine. So we vowed, "You are my love and you are important to me, and you will always be important to me."

Martha convinced her husband to move the family back near Iowa City, and eventually her marriage hit a decisive moment. Her husband found love letters from Dotty and demanded Martha break it off. Pulled between family and Dotty, she was devastated:

Martha: I was sitting at home on the couch crying one night, after he'd told me that, because I had been pretty much used to following what he said, you know? And my son came in, he was about twenty-one or twenty-two. He said, "What are you crying about?" And I said, "Oh, it's something that's goin' on with your dad and me." He

46

said, "Let's go out and get 31 Flavors and you can tell me about it."

So that was super. So we went out. He said "What'd he tell you that made you cry?" And I said (. . . Gee, it makes me cry to think about it . . .), "Your dad says I have to break it off with Dotty, and I just can't do that." And my son said, "Well, you know, if Dad told me that, that I had to break it off with somebody I liked, do you know what I'd tell him?" "No," I said. And my son said, "Two words: Fuck you!"

It was like a laser beam that came into my head: "That's true. He can't tell me what to do!" The next day I said to my husband, "I don't know what you have to do, but I know what I have to do. I have to be with Dotty."

Martha divorced her husband five years into the ten years it took before she and Dotty could live together. She moved back to Iowa City, got a job, rented an apartment, and the two spent two or three nights a week together. Eventually Dotty's youngest child graduated from high school, her primary responsibilities as a parent were over, and they moved in together.

Susan: Well, you know, this is a fabulous story, actually. Don't you feel lucky? Do you feel lucky?
Dotty: Oh yes, definitely.
Martha: Oh my gosh, yes.

Susan: Kind of a miracle.

Dotty: It was very traumatic, trying to get all of our marriages ended, because we had been raised in strict, traditional families, and. . . .

Susan: Whyever do you think it happened to you?

Martha: We fell in love, and it was just such a tremendously powerful force that there was no way that I felt we could ever have done anything else. I still feel that way, that there was no other way for us.

* * * * *

It is eighteen years since the spring that Martha and Dotty committed themselves to love each other forever, and ten years since they've been able to live together. Part of that powerful force that drew them together was, of course, sexual. Since they've lived together, sex has become less important in their lives. Martha analyzes it this way:

Martha: Love is three things, it's not one. It's the eros, the erotic stuff; it's the caring; and it's the decision.

The erotic stuff is very short. That intense stuff doesn't really last.

The caring is the opposite; it goes on forever.

And the third is the decision. The whole relationship is pretty much based on that. "Do you want to be together?" is a head thing, not a heart thing. It has nothing to

48

do with eros at all. "We want to be together" is a decision. Dotty and I made that decision along the way.

I reminded her of how compelling the attraction was, though, at the beginning:

> *Martha:* I think it was beyond our control at the beginning. And then as I began to understand it intellectually and accept it as a way of life, it became a choice. As the physical attraction began to lower, then it became a choice.

Now that Martha and Dotty live together, they find they have a good deal of conflict around how the household is run. After all, each was the boss of her own household for many years. When they can't compromise, for instance about how to decorate something, they just don't do anything for a while. Both are opinionated and stubborn: Dotty: "She feels that I am, and I feel that she is; she says that I make all the decisions, and I think she makes most of them . . ." Martha thinks that Dotty, having raised five children, just can't quite give up being a mother. Martha: "She appears to believe that her part of the relationship is to see that I do not make any mistakes."

Dotty has more income right now, and is paying about two-thirds of the costs of redecorating their house and some other extraordinary expenses. They split the ordinary expenses fifty-fifty.

They eat lunch out every day. Dotty: "We figured out that between the two of us we have cooked for other people for seventy-two years, and that's enough."

* * * * *

After Martha retired, three years ago, she and Dotty bought a tiny trailer and "we went out on the road." They traveled 48,000 miles.

Martha: We lived together in that little trailer, and most people say, "I don't know anybody else in the world that could do that for two years."
Susan: What an adventure!
Martha: Yeah, a tremendous adventure, after all those years of. . . .
Susan: Has it occurred to you that you lived your lives through once, and then you started over again at about age 16? I'm thinking of when you were giggling around together at that first conference. It's like two whole. . . .
Dotty: Oh yeah, two whole separate lives.

Chapter 2
Commitment

Prior Relationships

It is never too late to start a long-term lesbian relationship. Evelyn, age 69, has been in her present relationship for twenty-six years. Before that she was in six relationships that lasted four years, five years, two years, five, five, and five years; five of the six with women. The shortest, the two-year relationship, was the only one involving a man, and she was married to him. Her partner Patricia has been in only one significant relationship in her life, this one. She is 52, and was 26 when the relationship began.

The other women report similarly varied relationship histories. Women can come to long-term lesbian coupling from past experiences with either women, men or both; from many past experiences, or none; and can begin their long-term relationship at any age (The youngest woman in my sample began her current relationship at age 14; the oldest at age 57.)

Table 2.1 shows the sex of these lesbians' partners in prior significant relationships.

Slightly more than half the lesbians (52.3 percent) have intimate experience only with women. This means that close to half (47.7 percent) of the women in long-term lesbian couples have significant experience in prior relationships with men.

Twenty-seven percent (58 women) were married to these men. Seventy-three percent of the lesbians in long-term couples have never been married to a man.

TABLE 2.1 SEX OF PARTNERS IN PRIOR SIGNIFICANT RELATIONSHIPS

Sex of partner in prior relationship	Number of women	Percent of women
This is the first relationship	43	19.9
Prior only with women	70	32.4
Prior only with men	38	17.6
Prior with both men and women	65	30.1
Total	216	100.0

Do women with similar relationship histories pair with each other? No. Forty-nine couples share a similar relationship history as far as the sex of past partners is concerned. More than half the sample, 59 of the 108 couples, have dissimilar sex-of-partner relationship histories.

Nor are there patterns in the previous marital status of partners. In 55 percent of the couples neither woman has been married. Forty-three percent are couples where one woman has been married and the other has not. In only six couples have both women been married.

Thirty-one couples are made up of women who have experience only with other women. This is 29 percent of the sample. Seventy-one percent of the couples include at least one woman who has prior significant experience with men.

What I conclude from all this is:

Long-term lesbian couples in this study are made up of women who have a great deal of experience with prior relationships. Such experience is not critical to being in a long-term couple, however, because for a significant minority, 20 percent, this is their first relationship.

A large minority of the women who settle in long-term lesbian couples have considerable experience with men, often having been married to them. They are thus making an informed choice of an alternative to heterosexual relationships.

A majority of the women in this study have no experience with men that they consider significant. They knew what they wanted without having to sample the alternative at close range, or, more accurately, at any closer range than their family of origin.

Becoming a Couple

How did the women in long-term couples know they were a couple in the beginning? I asked: "What was it about your relationship — what happened — that made you begin to think of yourselves as a couple?"

"She moved in after the first date. What could I do?" (Carla, age 63, a 25-year couple)

"We were children, 14 and 17 years old. We started playing Dracula, and we realized that Dracula's kisses were getting rather passionate." (Marian, age 41, another 25-year couple)

Often, it is the experience of being sexual together that defines becoming a couple:

"We already loved each other, and it was the discovery that we wanted to and could make love together that made me realize we could be 'mates'" (Betsy, age 39, 21-year couple)

"We jumped on each other's bods, as virgins, and simply wanted to stay together. We didn't actually talk about 'marriage.' We just kept making love for a long time! We

accidentally did all the right things I guess."
(Jane, age 52, 31-year couple)

For other women, it's moving in together that is critical:

"Moving in together. It was the culmination of our courtship. We met, worked together (briefly), dated, then slept together, then moved in. If it had been legal, we would have gotten married." (Judith, age 37, 13-year couple)

Many different experiences can cause a pair to make the initial commitment of thinking of themselves as a couple. Some women are very intentional ("We drew up a 'contract' about our dreams, goals, and responsibilities as a committed couple."); others operational ("I'm observant. She was always there when I woke up and vice versa."); and some just throw themselves to the winds ("We fell desperately in love, passionately, unreasonably, obsessively.").

Some become a couple despite themselves:

"We used to talk about not being a couple and going out with other people, but neither of us were interested in going out, so after a time of being in denial about being a couple, it hit me that we were a couple (no matter what we said)." (Alison, age 34, 12-year couple)

Couples seem to experience their commitment in one of two ways: Either they remember themselves as coming together in a moment, or they perceive themselves as slowly evolving together over time. Everyone would agree that certain moments are significant, and alternatively, that commitment deepens with experience, but there are still two distinguishable camps.

Here's the story of a moment: "A Kirby vacuum salesman sold us 'the works' with both of our signatures and a big, common debt." (Carrie, age 60, 31-year couple)

By contrast Ellen and Frances are a couple of eighteen years who took the first six to get to the point of exchanging rings and making a commitment to work toward being able to live together sometime. During the first six years there was much emotional chaos and hurt. Frances: "The emotional anguish we went through . . . it was just crazy. We didn't even know what was right or wrong."

> *Ellen:* It wasn't going to last. There was no commitment.
> *Frances:* I never planned ahead, so I didn't know what to expect or what I was hoping for. I just lived the relationship as it was at the time.

Nine years after falling in love, three years after exchanging rings, this couple had struggled to get themselves to San Francisco. They moved in together:

> *Frances:* To me that was like a major surrender because I was always totally independent. It was scary because being committed has to do with the ultimate

acceptance of yourself by another person, but it felt great . . . Then we broke up again.

They lived apart in the same city while Ellen did intensive therapy and Frances pursued another woman. After a year they got back together and rented a house. The ultimate commitment was to come:

Frances: Do you know what precipitated the *real* commitment? Buying a washer and dryer.

Ellen: It was a major household purchase that we did together.

Frances: That's right. Together. Together we were in on this. And I had never, ever wanted anything that was gonna tie me down to any place. This was the ultimate in commitment.

Ellen: She always wanted to be able to put everything she owned in the back of her car.

Frances: And take off. I had done that for so long.

Ellen: So now we take all of our friends down in the basement and show them our commitment.

Why did Ellen and Frances not give up and do something easier with their lives?

Frances: Ellen opened me up as a person. When you discover the meaning of love, it's

just the most unique thing . . .
experiencing it, you know. Ellen was that
person for me.
Ellen: I'm an extremely loyal person, maybe
loyal to a fault. I'm determined.

Commitment Is a Spirit of Dedication

Whether the couples felt their commitment
immediately or developed the feeling over time, they
all agree feeling committed is important to staying
together. When asked what they felt were the three
most significant factors in staying together, the factor
ranked Most Significant overall was LOVE.

Maude, 78 years old, a 41-year couple: "1st most
significant: Love. 2nd most significant: Love. 3rd most
significant: Love."

The factor that ranked second was Common
Values/Goals/Interests (see Chapter 3).

The third factor was a tie between Being Friends
(see Chapter 4) and Commitment. This is how women
in long-term couples look at commitment:

"We've been determined to do whatever we
need to in order to meet the challenges and
overcome the obstacles — we really want to
grow old together." (Deborah, age 39, 13-year
couple)

"Commitment: Deciding from the outset
that we'd be 'married' and not just passing
through one another's lives." (Barbara, age 38,
12-year couple)

These women are talking about the attitude of commitment, a dedication of oneself to the idea that this relationship will last, despite problems that may — and will — come up.

"We have succeeded at crisis times in struggling to the point of deepening our intimacy and vulnerability. I think in large part because of our firm underlying commitment which supports us in looking for ways through difficulty rather than ways out via giving up." (Mary, age 39, 10-year couple)

Let me tell you what one couple was able to do because of their commitment. Mary Pat and Beryl have been together eighteen years. They live in Portland, Oregon in a working-class section of town. Four years into their relationship Beryl had an affair.

Beryl: I had an affair with a younger woman. It really shook our relationship up. It was extremely hard.

Mary Pat: We kept living together though.

Beryl: For about six months, we lived together, but we were just stagnant. It was like, ugh. But somehow, somehow we healed through that. I don't know how. We just kept . . . we didn't really talk much . . . we just lived together.

Mary Pat: Well, for one thing, you made a decision not to be involved with this person any more. I mean, that was necessary.

Beryl: We started mending, but the damage was there. You can't just say, "Oh, jeez,

I'm sorry." It's not quite that easy. But we started some of the preliminary kinds of things, and then we just let each other be and let each other mend a little bit. Then after those six months or so we started talking again. . . .

Mary Pat: If I'm really honest, part of my staying there was fear, you know. Even though it was really awful, I didn't want to be alone. I could have moved home: that would have been even more awful.

Beryl: Same here. Although I'd moved out of other relationships, and I still would move out of this one if I had to, I didn't want to. It just didn't feel like this relationship was finished.

They talk in more detail about how very difficult this period was. Then,

Mary Pat: I think it was just a matter of calming down too. And you have to decide. You have to make a decision. Are you going to trust this person again or not? Are you going to let your hurt go and let it heal, or are you going to keep it as this festering wound . . . and pull out all the time?

Beryl: We have a sense, and I think it's part of our value system, that life does go on and we will get through it, and gee, this is hard right now but . . . (Mary Pat: "It'll pass.") . . . It'll pass.

Commitment Is Interdependence

Commitment is an attitude, but not just an attitude. It is also a structure of mutual dependencies. All the long-term couples have created lives of interdependence. That's what being in a vital couple is, the gradual development of more and more intimate levels of intermingling.

From the first we abandon our emotional independence by falling in love. We give our loved one the power to bring us joy or misery. When we become lovers we give over more of our independence. Now our sexual partner has access to our bodies. She has the power to please us, and she enters that hidden world where all our sexual hangups live. With each orgasm — or lack thereof — we become increasingly emotionally dependent.

We also begin to express our relationship through practical arrangements in the outside world, arrangements that create external interdependency. We move in together, a major step. Of the 108 couples in my study, 106 live together full time.

Since they first moved in together, 59 percent of the couples have lived together full time without any substantial periods of separation. Twenty-four percent have been separated for six months or less and 6.5 percent for seven months to one year. Ten percent (eleven couples) have been separated for one year or more. The reasons involve work and school separations and "personal differences," which I defined as trial separations, breaking up, etc. (Eleven of the couples in the sample did maintain long trial separations or break up and get back together during the course of their long-term relationship.)

Buying a house together is another major step in interdependency and commitment. For 83 percent of the couples, either one of the women (12 percent) or both (71 percent) own their home. Five couples have some other arrangement, usually a third party who also owns a share. Only 12 percent (thirteen couples) are renting. And even this small number is misleading because some of those couples have owned homes together in the past, and have now either moved and will presumably buy again, or have retired and no longer want to maintain a house. Home ownership is distinctly the pattern of choice.

Because that first home is interpreted as a major step in commitment, it can be traumatic to a couple. Eleanor and Lori, an Arizona couple of eighteen years, commuted between each other's small towns for the first three years of their relationship. They then moved to Phoenix together and rented for a year.

> *Eleanor:* We really loved living together, our patterns are good together. And then after that first year we bought a house together and practically fell apart. There's something in buying, that commitment, that I've noticed in ourselves and other couples . . . you get real scared.
>
> *Susan:* What do you think is so scary?
>
> *Eleanor:* I was never interested in buying a house before. I really made a commitment when we bought the house, and it was suddenly the realization: I can't just walk out of this! I mean, I can walk out, but where's my money? Jeez! It was scary.
>
> *Lori:* It's the epitome of a ceremony, you

know. I mean, there is no other ceremony, so it's like, this is it. This is it.

A home is a particularly emotion-laden expression of practical commitment. The women mentioned other important expressions: wills, joint investments, powers of attorney, owning a business together, and, of course, sharing money.

Arrangements about Money

I asked "How do you and your partner handle your finances together? For example, do you share all your money, share some money, share no money, etc?" Then I asked the women to "describe in brief detail what arrangements you and your partner have made about handling money."

There are two principal ways long-term lesbian couples arrange their money (with variations given this is a creative group). Fifty-five percent share all their money:

"All our money and property have always been together." (Peggy, age 54, 17-year couple)

"What's mine is hers and what's hers is mine." (Ilona, age 50, 23-year couple)

"We consider our income to be collective income and spend it as such, though we keep separate checking accounts. We have discovered over time that she makes decisions about expenditures of less than $200 well, and I make decisions about expenditures of greater than $20,000 well. We have trouble with those in between." (Natalie, age 37, 13-year couple)

The other most popular arrangement, settled upon by 30.6 percent of the couples, is the following: both partners contribute equally to household accounts, and then each has her own money. Other expenses (vacations, gifts, etc.) are kept track of and the expenses shared equally. However, there is a lot of fuzziness about this arrangement:

"We each handle our own, but we are very loose about who pays what. Tends to be whoever has money at the moment. Also, I pay for home repair and materials, she tends to buy more food, but that varies too." (Margaret, age 35, a 10-year couple)

Even couples who try to keep things completely separate have trouble doing so consistently:

"We both contribute equally to a household checking account although my partner will purchase things for the home with her money. A list is kept of what belongs to who. We basically attempt to keep all of our finances separate, but this does not always work." (Sandy, age 34, 10-year couple)

The remaining 14 percent of the couples have a proportional money arrangement which reflects differences in their incomes: The partner who earns the most money contributes the most in some way. There are three principal proportional arrangements:

1. In six couples (5.6 percent) both partners contribute equally to household expenses; beyond that each woman has her own money; but the partner with the most money buys big items not included in the household budget, like vacations;
2. In five couples (4.6 percent) each contributes to the household in proportion to her income; then each woman has her own money; big items are paid for equally; and,
3. In four couples (3.7 percent) each contributes to the household in proportion to income; each then has her own money; and the partner with the most money buys the big items.

Although each couple has different arrangements, all the couples shared money to some degree. Those whom we might say shared the least, the 30 percent who contribute equally to a household account and maintain everything else separately, still pool their resources around this account, and have trouble keeping this pooling from creeping into other aspects of their lives together. Seventy percent either pool everything, or pool according to some proportional agreement.

The impression I have, both from the questionnaires and the interviews, is that money is not a source of difficulty and friction for lesbian couples who've been together as long as ten years. Whatever problems may have been present in the past have been resolved for most of these couples. What problems remain reflect lack of money for the couple as a whole or one partner feeling she does not contribute her share. What is important here in a discussion about commitment is that all these couples have intertwined their resources to some degree.

Children and Others

Many lesbian couples care for children, a clear instance of practical commitment. One couple who've been together eleven years and have two adopted children consider these children among the three most significant factors that explain why they have stayed together:

Factor:
1. We love each other.
2. We made a commitment, so if things get rough we work it out.
3. The kids. The kids took all the pettiness out of our lives. We became real, a family.
4. The dogs. (Sally, age 42)

Her partner agrees:

2. Mutual commitment, to each other, the kids, the dogs, the house. (Robin, age 39)

For those women who have them, the presence of children undoubtedly creates interdependencies and loyalties that cannot be shrugged off lightly.

Likewise the dogs. There is no question that pets

are very important to many lesbian couples. Many interviews were done with a cat or two sitting on the dining room table amongst the coffee cups, muffins, questionnaires, and tape recorder. Women mention the importance of their pets when talking about the joys and pleasures of their relationship,

> "The joy of having someone to share my life with. There are too many pleasures — walking on our beach gathering fireplace bark and watching the dog gambol. Climbing into bed each night to the warmth and comfort of the other's body. . . ."

or when adding their own comments at the end of the questionnaire:

> "I think it would be interesting to see how many lesbian couples have pets, cats or dogs. We have two cats and they are a big part of our household."

Other Types of Formal Commitment

Three-quarters of the women in long-term lesbian couples have made a formal commitment of some sort to each other. Table 2.2 reports this information.

Clearly, the type of formal commitment most of us choose is a verbal agreement. The second most popular is exchanging rings. About a third of us have created some kind of formal ceremony, perhaps just between the two of us, but nonetheless as an intentional expression of commitment. Several couples

TABLE 2.2 TYPE OF FORMAL COMMITMENT

Type of commitment	Number of couples	Percent of couples
Verbal agreement	64	78.0
Written agreement	8	9.8
Ceremony between the two of us	15	18.3
Ceremony involving friends	9	11.0
Ceremony involving clergy	4	4.9
Ceremony in church	2	2.4
Exchanged rings	43	52.4

Note: The numbers and percentages total more than 100 because the same couple may have done several things.

have had formal ceremonies involving others. The ceremony of a thirteen-year couple was presided over by a Dignity (Catholic) priest and attended by friends. Another couple had a Holy Union to celebrate their twentieth anniversary (they've now been together thirty years) at their city's Metropolitan Community Church, a Protestant gay church. A woman pastor presided and women friends came to acknowledge and support their commitment.

A twelve-year couple, Laura and Robin, participated in a collective trysting ceremony, a unique part of which was a commitment that ". . . it's not that you're going to stay together for the rest of your lives, but that if you break up you're not going to trash each other, kill each other, be mean to each other; you're going to remain friends. You may not always be lovers, but you'll always be friends." (Robin, age 44)

Such ceremonies bring up the question of anniversaries. Most long-term couples celebrate an anniversary, some several. The small number who do not may omit such celebrations intentionally, e.g., they are superstitious that celebrating their commitment may endanger it. Or they may be the kind of people who don't much like ceremonies of any kind. Those who do celebrate anniversaries are faced with a problem: which of the significant comings-together in their evolving couple experience should they call their anniversary? The most common choices are: the first time the women were sexual together; when they moved in together; when they bought a house together; or when they had some kind of ceremony. Typical are Laura and Robin who celebrate two anniversaries, one when they became lovers, the second for their trysting.

A Word About Emotional Interdependence

We've been talking about the practical interdependencies lesbians create which both express or symbolize their commitment and simultaneously strengthen that commitment: buying a house, investing together, owning a business together, having powers of attorney to care for each other, sharing money, caring for children and pets. I want to end, though, where we began, by talking about emotional interdependence.

As I read her questionnaire, a woman in a fourteen-year relationship startled me by attributing her staying with her partner most importantly to co-dependence. She elaborated:

"I have found out recently about my dysfunctional family situation as a child, about addictive behavior, about co-dependence. I see that those symptoms and behaviors are part of having stayed in this relationship, and I'm thankful to be able to see those things as pluses. For as we both deal with our individual lives together, we can appreciate and support ourselves, each other, and our relationship all the more." (Lucy, age 45)

Somehow this woman — and presumably her therapist — have been able to define Lucy's co-dependence as having been positive for her and her relationship. Lucy is appreciating the bond that such patterns can forge, even if, apparently, the time has come for some change.

Whether or not they are technically co-dependent (the psychological profession offers a variety of definitions of this phenomenon), many of the women in this study are unashamedly dependent on each other. They do everything together.

"I can't even go potty unless I tell her I'm goin'. Let's face it . . . We do everything together. We just love being together. We don't care if we never have company. We just enjoy each other." (Norma, age 67, 32-year couple)

Many women say: "I can't imagine living without her." They wear each other's clothes and drive each other's cars. This is Kate and Marilyn, a nineteen-year couple, explaining how few things they don't share:

Susan: How separate do you keep your things?
Kate: Well, our underwear is the same. I mean we have nothing separate, really.
Marilyn: That's an exaggeration. We decided we should keep our underwear separate. We wear different size bras, so that's why.
Kate: I wear all white.
Marilyn: I wear colored.
Kate: We really share everything, unless it's impractical to share it. You know, you tend to walk differently in your shoes, so we tend not to share shoes.
Marilyn: We wear the same size, but we do walk differently.
Kate: We're not really hung up on ownership.
Marilyn: We're really not.

Obviously, some women can tolerate and enjoy very high levels of togetherness. Many seek out and flourish under what might seem extremely enmeshed lives. If these women are happy, how are we to evaluate the warnings we hear about being fused or co-dependent?

To me, it seems a matter of degree and a matter of personal tolerance. We are all dependent on other people, and most particularly dependent on our partners, dependent for attention, for honesty, for respect, for love. What our partner says, how she feels, what she does is critical to us emotionally.

I fear we too often slip into stigmatizing commitment and loyalty and self-sacrifice as fusion or being co-dependent without being careful about the very particular — and extreme — problem co-dependency addresses.

71

The best definition I've heard of co-dependency is: "the chronic neglect of self in favor of something or someone else." The key word is chronic. We need to put our partners first sometimes, but not all the time. One woman talks about this danger when she offers advice:

> Knowing what you want and need in a relationship is important. And valuing yourself too. Often women need to learn these basics. The ways women were/are raised contributes to this undervaluing of ourselves. You think everyone's needs but yours are important." (Julie, age 44, 15-year couple)

So we need to beware of the chronic neglect of self. We need to put ourselves first sometimes.

But not all the time. There is no reason our lesbian community should embrace unfettered independence in an attempt to avoid being co-dependent. True, living entirely for someone else and never for yourself is no doubt unhealthy. (The second best definition I ever heard of co-dependence is: You know you're co-dependent when you're drowning and someone else's life flashes before you.) But living as if no one else could desperately matter to you is probably pathological and surely lonely.

Commitment is about putting your life and love in someone else's hands.

Conclusions

Long-term lesbian couples achieve commitment by

developing a certain attitude and by creating the conditions of interdependence.

I think the attitude of commitment has two interrelated basic tenets: (1) the belief that you will stay together ("We have the assumption that we will be together, not that we will split up."); and (2) the understanding that the relationship will persist despite difficult times.

The first of these is an article of faith, a matter of choosing to believe.

The second is a recognition of the realities of life with another person. Life is difficult. The lesbian couples who stay together do not have things easier than other couples. Things have gotten hard for them too, sometimes very hard.

It's easy to stay together when things are going great. Whoever broke up during the honeymoon? It's when things feel terrible and are terrible that our commitment becomes relevant. Being committed says this: You and I will stay together even — perhaps especially — when we don't want to. Or rather, when we don't want to keep struggling, we will remember that: (1) our relationship is, at its heart, satisfying to both of us; (2) things will get better; and (3) we have a commitment to working toward that better time ("Commitment to each other through good and bad — forever.").

Postscript: Dating and Commitment — A Cautionary Note

A woman in a thirteen-year couple observes, "Many women's relationships are defined as relationships before the people know each other very well." She feels this is a reason lesbian relationships may not last. Another woman, also in a thirteen-year couple says, "I think too many women think of themselves as a couple when they should just be dating, and thus break up."

What this suggests is that too often lesbians confuse dating and commitment. We think of ourselves as "married," and thus suffer from a high "divorce" rate, when what we really are doing when we go in and out of relationships is dating. It doesn't look like dating, however, because we've moved in together. We find ourselves living with someone and think we must be committed to them, or should be. Then, when we get to know them a bit, we find they aren't the right person. We break up, but not easily or with any grace.

This lack of clear dating behavior, I believe, is in part a consequence of being unable to legally marry. We do not have access to a conventional social form that defines and legitimizes commitment. As a result, there is no demarcation between choosing to commit oneself to a partner and simply sampling what potential partners might have to offer. Some of us are able to make a considered commitment despite this, but for many, I think, our commitments are inadvertent. We have difficulty knowing what commitment is because we slip into it unintentionally.

I believe some change needs to happen. We need to make dating and choosing to be committed separate stages of a relationship. Where in this process we put moving in together is critical, since that step is often interpreted as establishing a commitment, both by the women involved and by the outside lesbian world.

When I asked, "What advice do you have for other women who want to stay together?" Cynthia advised:

"Be honest. Make a commitment based on love, not infatuation. Be her best friend before you become her lover. Take your time and don't rush into a commitment." (age 37, 17-year couple)

Many of us don't know when we're dating or when we're committing to a long-term relationship because the two are so merged. One woman experienced a variation on this theme. She wanted to think she was *only* dating, because the idea of committing was too shameful.

Andrea, now 37, said when she first fell in love eighteen years ago with the woman who became her partner, the idea that their relationship was just a fling, that it was not serious, helped calm her internalized homophobia:

"I was in total shock, and when I did give the relationship any kind of guiltful thought — of course I was very guilty about it — I said to myself, 'This isn't going to last, so what difference does it make? . . . I don't need to worry too much because it's not going to last, and it'll be a nice experience for me.' "

If others feel like Andrea, they may avoid the idea of commitment because they're still too homophobic to admit that an interest in women could be anything more than fleeting, "just a phase."

I began this chapter on commitment by saying: It's never too late to become a long-term couple. Now we see that — for some — it can be too early. We may need to get used to the idea of being lesbian before we can commit wholeheartedly to being lesbian with one other woman. We may want to experience ourselves with different women, to dip in and out of relationships, to be bi-sexual, to maintain multiple relationships, to be celibate, all as experiments in how we will express our lesbian identity most comfortably. Choosing to be in a long-term couple is just one way of expressing that identity.

STORY 3:

LOUISE (age 39) & BETSY (age 39: 21 years together

Louise and Betsy are each other's first significant relationship. They met in college, fell in love, and became lovers, all without having any idea what was going on. They were total innocents.

Betsy: Neither of us had any idea what lesbianism was.

Louise: I used to get really upset and be crying and have kind of a strange feeling when Betsy would go out with other friends, but I couldn't figure out why. Sometimes I would say, "Well, I love Betsy." My friends would comfort me — missing the point, of course — they'd say: "That's okay, you can love her. We love her too."

Betsy: We didn't know anything about it. And as a result, we weren't threatened by it, we didn't try to hide anything. I remember in my single dorm room, we'd come back from class and just leave the door open. Louise would take her dress off and be in her slip and get in bed with me and take a nap.

Louise: The door's just hanging open!

Betsy: Now we think probably other people were aware; we were the ones who weren't. What did our friend Midge used to say? "Ah, the innocence of it all!"

Susan: Had you been sexual yet with each other?

Betsy: One spring we went to a party off campus. I had too much to drink, and suddenly something clicked, some insight. I thought: this person that I like so much could be my life mate. And at the same time I wanted to kiss her and stuff.

Susan: So it was like the sexuality part — the romantic part — and the life-long part sprang together into your mind?

Betsy: Yeah. Before that we were just really good friends, and really liked each other, but it didn't mean anything. It couldn't mean anything.

Susan: So what did you do?

Betsy: That first night, after everything hit me, I kept saying to Louise, "Tonight, okay? Tonight, okay?" I kept saying it, and passed out.

Susan: Did you know what she meant?

Louise: I couldn't have put it into words, but yeah, I knew what she was talking about.

Susan: So then what did you do? Make love in your dorm room?

Both: Yeah.

Susan: I remember exactly how that feels, not having any words for what you're doing, not even knowing that what you're doing can be done . . . how you can know things and not know things and do things and not put them into words . . . it's a miracle, really.

Louise: There were lots of things we didn't know. I didn't know anything about sex. I didn't know what orgasm was. She did, but she didn't bother to tell me.

Louise and Betsy have been together 21 years. They're turning 40 and live in a modern house in a semirural, semisuburban small development outside Sacramento, California. Louise teaches elementary kids, Betsy high school. Betsy is Welsh and English, Louise is Japanese.

I asked what being different races has meant to them. We discussed it in context of how their families reacted.

Susan: Was the different race part relevant to your families?

Betsy: No. Once they got used to the woman part, they were fine with the race part. They've actually been very supportive of our relationship. Both our families have been.

Louise: It wasn't a big thing for my family either. Other people, like my sister, are married to Caucasians. I'm more white, I think, than Japanese. I knew I was Japanese, but didn't think of myself as an outcast or any kind of minority, so it didn't dawn on me, you know, the fact that Betsy's white.

Betsy and Louise are also from different class backgrounds. Betsy's father managed a chain of retail stores; Louise's father was a broccoli farmer.

Susan: Have your different class backgrounds been important to you?

Betsy: I think it's been an attraction for both of us, certainly for me. My dad and I were really close, closer than either of us was with anybody else in the family. He grew up on a farm, and I used to love his stories about my grandfather and the farm. Louise would tell me the same stories, about her father and their farm. So her background is my dad's background. It seems like the same, the essence of what's there is the same, just two different generations.

Louise: The values of both families were the same: you work hard to get what you want.

Like other couples, Louise and Betsy's relationship has its own unique blend of differences and commonalities. Many couples say that one of the most significant factors helping them stay together are their common values, interests, goals, etc. Betsy puts it this way (she's responding to the question about the three most significant factors that explain why they've stayed together): "3. A common love of home and 'family' (two miniature collies) and work that allows us to make a warm, satisfying, productive, and loving home together."

Betsy and Louise share this love of home, but agree it is Louise who makes the home:

> "Home, that's my thing really. I want it to be nice and comfortable and lots of food and, you know, a happy place to be. Some people, they're never home, they never stay home because it isn't anything; they haven't made it into anything; it's not a neat place to be. But I love to be home. I love to come home, and I think Betsy's the same way."

This love of home, of the home Louise makes and Betsy loves, has a twist, though, a conflict of values that has plagued their relationship from the beginning. Louise's love of home also means she is perfectly happy being home with Betsy and their dogs. She is satisfied to meet all her needs for closeness and intimacy through Betsy. Betsy wants intimate friends outside the relationship.

> *Betsy:* That was kind of an unresolved problem for a long time. I didn't feel that I had

friends. You seemed to be fine without them, to be fine with a combination of your family and friends at work . . .

Louise: And just acquaintances. We're very different in that way. Because I grew up on the farm, I used to play a lot by myself or with my brother or my sister, and I was just perfectly happy. Every once in a while I'd have friends over, but I guess I like my own company. I mean, I'm satisfied.

Susan: Do you think anything about how you feel is relevant to Japanese culture?

Louise: I don't know.

Betsy: I think so.

Louise: I guess so. I know my family is that way. Just kind of satisfied, just with the family or just by yourself. I'm not anti-social or anything, but if we have people over, fine; if we don't, fine. Whereas Betsy really likes to see people.

Betsy: I can begin to resent her family, if I think it's just her family that is like this. It's easier if I think of it as being about being Japanese.

Louise: I don't know whether it's just my family. I think it's kind of all of them. None of those Japanese families have parties or are real social or anything.

Susan: Is this still a difference between you?

Betsy: I think it's still a difference. Even though I have friends that I like now, lots of times I want Louise to be with me to go somewhere, and you'd rather stay home. So it's kind of us pulling in different directions all the time. But it's a lot more resolved than it used to be.

I realize part of it's just me, that I'm too shy sometimes to go do something by myself.

Susan: Well, that's part of why you're in a couple, right? For the companionship of it. Imagine being out there trying to date, all on your own?

Louise: You'd probably like that, wouldn't you, Betsy?

Susan: Does it sound fun?

Betsy: Yeah, parts of it. But . . . I love to come home.

If you can detect a note of bitterness in Louise's last remark, you've picked up on something that is also true of Louise and Betsy's relationship. Betsy's attraction to other people is an ingredient in this story of how their differences and commonalities are intertwined. Let me try to explain how this works in their couple.

Nothing difficult in a relationship is ever so simple as to be "just" a racial/cultural difference, or "just" a personality difference, or "just" a matter of preference. Louise's love of home and wanting to be home and not being interested in outside intimate friendships has much to do with her Japanese culture, her family, and her personality. Betsy's wanting outside intimate friendships has much to do with her Caucasian willingness to reveal herself to strangers, her sociable family, and her personality. But these racial/cultural, familial, and personal differences are reinforced and exacerbated — made

83

complex and compelling — by Betsy's history of affairs. As she says, she keeps testing the relationship: "I keep testing it again and again. And it keeps coming out to be the best."

They recounted to me a sixteen-year history (beginning around their fourth year together) of Betsy's sexual interest in other people: "That was why I moved out sometimes, to see if I liked being straight, or to see if I liked some other kind of woman that lived differently. It always turned out awful." The longest outside relationship lasted seven years, with a male co-worker. There were many other, short relationships with women.

At the end of their tale I asked Louise how she could be so accepting of what must have been very painful.

> *Susan:* A lot of people would have been jealous and miserable and mad and said, "I don't want to see you any more," and that's it.
> *Betsy:* You were jealous and miserable and mad.
> *Louise:* Yeah, but I just never believed in what she was doing. I just didn't think that she really knew what she was doing, and I thought I was right. It sounds real conceited, but, you know, I just didn't think it was what she really wanted.
>
> So I would be mad and jealous. I mean we used to have some real fights, but I just survived. And you would kind of figure out that it wasn't what you wanted, but that didn't stop you from trying, from still testing and exploring. I really didn't

understand why it was going on, I just did not understand. But I just believed in us so much . . . I just believed that it would work out.

There is thus an added dimension to this couple's disagreement about the place of friends in their relationship. Clearly, Betsy's propensity for sexual entanglements with friends would not endear Louise to the idea of "intimate friends," an idea she doesn't care about in the first place.

At about the twenty-year mark in their relationship, however, everything may have changed. Louise called a halt:

Louise: The last time I just felt like I'd done this I can't even remember how many times. And it just came to me finally, after twenty years, you know, I just couldn't do it anymore. So I had to say that.

Betsy: The most recent word is that if I do that again, Louise is leaving, or I'm leaving this house, or something. So it was kind of an ultimatum.

You know, I think about it a lot. The affairs all seem to be bad experiences anyway. There seems to be something negative and bad and wrong. But then at other times I think, Well, what is wrong with it if you like somebody else and they're attractive? I think, am I ever going to be close to anybody but Louise again in my whole life? And what's the big deal?

I'm hoping that if I find, or if we

together can find friends, that might take care of whatever that urge is that keeps me getting involved with other people.

Louise: To help, I tried to find some other people and get more involved with them.

Susan: What's amazing to me . . .

Betsy: . . . is that we're still together! (Laughter)

Susan: That's exactly right. It is. Because those two orientations are so different. So how come you're still together?

Betsy: We love each other.

Louise: I don't know. I think I've always just felt like, you know, she said she loved me, and (she turns to Betsy) you're gonna stick by it, that's all. I believe you.

Louise and Betsy are each other's first significant relationship, and I think this fact helps explain how they can have survived this protracted source of pain for their relationship.

Two things occur to me. Lesbians who fell in love as teenagers, as youngsters really, and who have stayed together, have done all their growing up within the context of that one relationship. Many of us have grown up through a process of experimentation and change that we feel necessitated discarding relationships along the way. They stayed together, and have thus had to grow up right in each other's faces. I am not surprised that sometimes the process is chaotic and extraordinarily painful. The miracle is that they persist.

My second thought. We all know the power that very first attraction to a woman had for us. Many of us move on to other women and other relationships, but in our heart we may still have a special place for that very first love, that very first taste of passion. Louise and Betsy — and others in the study who are each other's first loves — have maintained that original bond. They still love, and make a life with, the woman they first loved. Who knows what powers of forgiveness and renewal flow from that connection.

Betsy: ". . . Just the way we talk to each other; it's like being home."

Chapter 3
Sameness/Difference

The Idea of Sameness

Lesbian couples are, by definition, two women together. This is our most obvious, and certainly our most profound, similarity. We are the same sex as our partner. "Lesbians are having a relationship with the same species, so to speak." (Nancy, age 41, fifteen-year couple)

This means we have all the qualities of women — whether bestowed by nature or by society — doubled.

When being female favors us with positive, helpful attributes, we have them in profusion. We are both potentially nurturant, nest-building, sharing, supportive, communicative, intimate, gentle, peaceful, equal. Doris: "I think of women as the superior gender: more stable, more sane, more social." A lesbian couple is blessed with *two* stable, sane, social creatures.

There is a flip side. When being female burdens us with negative qualities, the misfortunes are multiplied. We are both insecure, ashamed, misogynist, passive, masochistic, controlling, perfectionist and pre-menstrual. A lesbian couple is cursed with *two* crazed co-dependents

While these descriptions may strike you as stereotypes, I think there is no question that a complex commingling of natural and societal forces has created two sexes with distinctively different characters. As lesbians we glory in and suffer from what is true of women's character. We have, after all, chosen to love women, at least in part because we love what women are like. What a lesbian relationship gives us is what women are like — magnified by two.

We are talking here about similarities that all women would share to a greater or lesser degree, depending upon individual differences, of course. There are other similarities that only certain women share, particularities of attitude and behavior that are crucial to how two women will relate to each other.

The women in long-term couples see the similarities they share with their partners as extremely important to the longevity of their relationships. You remember that I asked about "the three most significant factors that explain why you have stayed together." Next to Love (always Number One in our woman's heart), the factor mentioned most often is Common Values, Goals, Interests: "Similar warped senses of humor, and similar ranges of good/bad taste." (a twelve-year couple) "Same values, e.g., monogamy and Christianity." (thirteen years)

I also asked, "What do you think forms the heart of a successful relationship?" Here again many women cited something to do with similarities: "Similar goals, life outlook." (a twelve-year couple) "Similar views on finances, politics, employment, family, friends . . . or a genuine willingness to accommodate/bend." (sixteen years together.)

Robin gives us a sense of how important similarities are in balancing our differences:

> "Although we are part of a couple, we have maintained our separate identities. We are both committed to feminism which has given us a very strong bond. About a lot of things we have very dissimilar likes and dislikes, which could have created problems. However, our agreement about politics and our respect for our differences has given us an important bond.
> We also share the same work place, which has been important." (age 44, a 12-year couple)

Robin and her partner are one couple among many in the group who consider themselves feminists. I asked several questions about these lesbians' attitudes toward politics and religion, to see what attitudes they have, and what attitudes they share with their partners. I asked, for example: "How sympathetic do you feel towards the feminist movement?" The women could then circle the answer that most closely represented their feelings/opinions on a nine-point scale that looked like this:

Extremely   *Not at all*
sympathetic   *sympathetic*
   1   2   3   4   5   6   7   8   9

The lesbians in this study are very sympathetic toward the feminist movement, with an average score of 1.85. Fully 90 percent of the women were quite sympathetic, responding with a 1, 2, or 3. Only two women said they were unsympathetic, responses 7, 8, or 9. The women are equally sympathetic to the lesbian/gay rights movement, with an average score for the group of 1.79. Again, 90 percent of the women responded with a 1, 2, or 3 in answer to this question. Six women said they were unsympathetic.

The other attitude questions were:

How religious would you say you are now?
Average = 6.98.
How spiritual would you say you are now?
Average = 4.64.
How would you describe your political outlook?
Average = 2.82, (where 1 = Extremely liberal to 9 = Extremely conservative).

The lesbians in long-term relationships come from mostly Western religions. The group as a whole is not very religious now, though religion is very important to a few women. The group is somewhat more spiritual (the distinction has to do with organized, traditional religion versus some more new age, radical, perhaps feminist form of worship).

The group is politically very liberal. Three-quarters of the women (76.9 percent) responded with a 1, 2, or 3 to the question "How would you describe your political outlook?" (1 = Extremely liberal). Only 4.2 percent consider themselves fairly conservative, responses 7, 8, or 9 (9 = Extremely conservative).

Since we are talking about similarities here, I compared how each partner in a specific couple answered the attitude questions to arrive at a measure of how much agreement there is within couples. This scale runs from 1 = Close agreement to 4 = Disagreement.

The couples are in fairly close agreement with each other on all five of the attitude items. Table 3.1 reports the degree of agreement. (The mean in this case indicates the amount of agreement, not the direction of the agreement, i.e., we cannot tell whether the partners are agreeing to be politically

TABLE 3.1 DEGREE OF AGREEMENT ON ATTITUDES

Attitude	Mean
Lesbian/Gay sympathy	1.27
Political identification	1.37
Feminism	1.43
Religion	1.69
Spirituality	1.95

liberal or conservative, just that they are in fairly close agreement about their political attitudes.)

Lesbian couples are in fairly close agreement on all five of these attitude items. There is more agreement within the couples about their attitudes toward the lesbian/gay movement than any of the other areas of agreement/disagreement. The least agreement is about the partners' attitudes toward spirituality.

Couples Who Value Closeness

For some of the couples, the entire relationship mirrors this kind of agreement about attitudes; the relationship is very close. One couple, Valerie and Gretchen, have been together seventeen years and are each other's first, and only, significant relationship. Gretchen, now 45, defines a significant relationship as "one in which I share myself and everything I possess with my partner forever."

I asked a series of four questions to try to get at how merged or separate the couples were. (Some of the psychological literature on lesbians worries about how merged or fused we are.) All the women responded to the question: "How important are each of the following to you . . ?" on a nine-point scale running from: 1 = Extremely important to 9 = Not at all important. Table 3.2 gives you the items, the average response for all the women, and the responses of Valerie and Gretchen.

Clearly, women in couples where closeness is a high value — women like Valerie and Gretchen —

94

TABLE 3.2 COMPARISON OF GROUP MEANS WITH THOSE OF A "CLOSE COUPLE" ON "MERGED" QUESTIONS

Question: How important is it to you . . .	Group mean	Valerie's score	Gretchen's score
Spending as much time together with my partner as possible	2.79	1.0	1.0
Sharing as many activities with my partner as possible	3.13	1.0	1.0
Having major interests of my own outside the relationship	4.02	3.0	8.0
Having a group of friends to support me in addition to partner's support	4.03	6.0	8.0

differ from the group as a whole when we look at these "Merged" items.

Valerie and Gretchen share all their money, own their home together, work in similar managerial jobs, and have never been apart for any length of time. They are closeted with respect to everyone except other lesbians. They are somewhat active in the lesbian community, subscribe to lesbian journals, and are open with other lesbians. They are clearly ambivalent about their contacts with other lesbians, however, because Gretchen thinks the main reason they've stayed together is: "Being isolated from the lesbian community."

Valerie and Gretchen are sexual about once a month and are monogamous. They perceive almost complete equality in their relationship; "Equality was never a big problem. We have encouraged each other to grow in all aspects of our lives." Neither perceives any sources of problems.

I asked "What are the most joyful things about your relationship as a whole; what gives you the most pleasure?"

> *Valerie:* Knowing that there will be someone there to share your feelings each day, someone to laugh with, cry with, and be tender with.
> Seeing my lover happy and knowing that she will always love me gives me the most pleasure.
> *Gretchen:* Seeing my partner happy.

At the end of the questionnaire Valerie volunteers:

> "I feel that one of the main reasons our relationship has lasted is because we have not allowed outside forces to share our problems. When we are having difficulties, we look to each other to work them out; we don't let everyone know when things are not going well with us. We set aside time each week just for us. No one or nothing else is to interfere with that time.
> I truly wish everyone could have a love as great as mine . . . We have a fairytale (no pun intended) relationship and both feel very blessed that we found each other.

Let me introduce you to one more such close

couple, Ginny and Virginia, who've been together twenty-three years. They are in their early fifties, both early retirees from many years working for Boeing, Ginny for twenty-eight years, Virginia for nineteen. They live in Seattle, in a house they built themselves.

They described to me a jealous, drunken, physical fight they had ten years into their relationship, their one and only huge fight. ("We let ten years come out.") I asked why they thought they hadn't broken up around this fight:

> *Virginia:* I have always felt, when I started going with Ginny, that I would live with her the rest of my life; I didn't care what happened.
>
> *Ginny:* Because I love her so much . . . This is it for the rest of my life . . . For sure we have our disagreements, but they should be so severe they would break us up?

Later I asked them why they think they've stayed together:

> *Ginny:* We like to do absolutely everything together. Everything. We worked in the same room together for three years at Boeing, just the two of us. Ate lunch together. How we ever survived it, no one can understand. But when she's not around me, I'm lost. I guess I'm a little weird that way . . . I really can't stand it when she's not around.

Virginia: A lot of people say to us: "I don't see how you did it. I have to have *my* space." Well, I just don't want that.

Ginny: So if anything ever happens to her, I don't know what's gonna happen to me . . . (she thinks about death) I go first, it's a deal.

I always asked women whether there were things about each other they wanted to change when they first got together, and how this matter of changing each other had worked out:

Ginny: There was nothing about Virginia that I thought I would change. I was hoping maybe she'd change a few things about me, which she did.

Virginia: What did I change about you?

Ginny: Well, you know, I was a little wild and crazy.

Virginia: Well, you're still wild and crazy!

Ginny: I didn't want to change a thing about her.

Virginia: I didn't want to change Ginny either.

Later, I return to this.

Susan: You said you were hoping Virginia would change something about you.

Ginny: Well, it was the fact that I liked to party too much . . . All my life I've enjoyed my beer, probably more so than I should have. But it hasn't gotten me in that much trouble.

Susan: So you were hoping that Virginia would calm you?

Ginny: Yeah.

Susan: Do you think that's happened?

Ginny: That's happened. She was pretty quiet too, when I first met her. Didn't say too much. So I drew her out, and then she calmed me down. So it worked out.

These couples are examples of many women in the group who enjoy high levels of closeness. They contrast with others who are much more separate.

Couples Who Value Separateness

For some couples being separate, developing and maintaining a clear sense of their individuality within the context of their coupleness, is critical to their long-term relationship.

One such couple, Margaret and Leah, are not as different as the couple I will introduce later, but their relationship has a distinctly different tone from those of the "Close Couples." They have been together ten years, but lived separately for the first nine. This is the only couple of the 108 who lived apart so long: "We preferred it that way. I wanted my own place as I'm a writer." They lived a block apart, each in one-bedroom apartments, and went back and forth, spending almost every night together. Though they contribute equally to their house account, beyond that they make all financial decisions separately. One woman is Jewish, the other Protestant (Church of England).

But there are similarities. Both are in their early forties, have post college degrees, and work in some aspect of book publishing. Their incomes are similar, and they have agreed to be monogamous.

As you would expect, they score differently on the "Merged" questions than the group as a whole, though not extremely so. Table 3.3 compares the group means on these questions with Margaret's and Leah's responses, so you can see how different they are. (1 = Extremely important; 9 = Not at all important.)

Margaret's scores indicate that she feels "Spending time with her partner" is a bit more important than the group as a whole. But "Sharing activities" is less

TABLE 3.3 COMPARISON OF GROUP MEANS WITH THOSE OF A "SEPARATE COUPLE" ON "MERGED" QUESTIONS

Item	Group mean	Margaret's scores	Leah's scores
Spending as much time together with my partner as possible	2.79	2	5
Sharing as many activities with my partner as possible	3.13	5	5
Having major interests of my own outside the relationship	4.02	2	1
Having a group of friends to support me in addition to partner's support	4.03	2	1

important, and "Having major interests" and a "Group of friends" is distinctly more important.

Leah's scores show even more "separateness." "Spending time with her partner," and "Sharing activities" is only moderately important. "Having major interests" and a "Group of outside friends" is extremely important.

It is noteworthy that couples where both partners emphasize separateness share this value. They are similar in the extent to which they value independence. Imagine trying to pair Ginny (a partner in a Close Couple) and Leah. Ginny would likely feel chronically abandoned; Leah suffocated. They might work something out, but the match would not look like a good one for starters.

The advice Margaret and Leah offer has to do with independence. Margaret: "Don't try if you don't have a really strong bond to start with. Have independent lives. Learn to be apart, even when it's frightening." Leah: "Choose a partner carefully. Maintain separate identities."

This couple has a blend of separateness and closeness. They worked to develop and maintain a sense of independence ("Learn to be apart, even when it's frightening."), and have over the years evolved into an interdependent unit. Leah responds to the "Three Most Significant Factors" question:

> "We each wanted to learn something very important from the other. We were each highly developed in certain areas and grossly underdeveloped in others. And we each had what the other lacked."

Leah also describes what has helped keep them together:

"We have become family to each other, as well as lovers and best friends. And that sense of being family (neither of us has much of any other family) has become potent."

Margaret and Leah are a moderately separate couple. Margery and Kathryn are a very separate couple. They have lived together for twenty-four years. They are the only couple (they *are* a couple in my opinion) who denied or were unsure about whether they are a couple. I asked "Do you and your partner consider yourselves a couple?" Margery: "No. Two people. Couple of what? Our friends and others consider us a couple no doubt." Kathryn: "What is meant by 'couple'?" They do not celebrate an anniversary. They do, however, agree they have never considered dissolving the relationship (Breaking up was "never a serious possibility") and that they are permanently committed to each other: Margery: "In the sense that we will live with and care for each other till death, as far as we can predict, 'one day at a time.'"

Margery is 71 years old, Kathryn 69. Both women were raised in liberal Protestant religions, are highly educated, and worked full-time in different professions until their recent retirement. They share some household expenses, but keep track of whose money is whose. One woman owns the house and cars, the other pays rent and all expenses on the cars.

They both consider their relationship equal, and feel that this equality is important to it, though

Margery points out that they have different approaches in exerting their power and influence: "I'm more devious; she's more adamant." They share some basic values, like an intense love of nature and a commitment to honesty. But they emphasize their differences: of class, income, savings and spending habits, tasks around the house, and their attitudes toward children.

What is unique about this relationship and contributes to its intensely separate feel is that Margery and Kathryn have been celibate with each other for twenty of their twenty-four years ("We probably had sex together in our whole twenty-four years maybe ten times."). They've had lots of physical affection ("We've had lots of caressing, we kiss each other and hug each other . . ."), but hardly any sex. During this long time together, both have had significant and prolonged sexual relationships with other women, friends who are very important to each of them, some of whom amount to an extended family.

> *Margery:* Basically our relationship is not sexual. There was a brief flurry that wasn't really that important, and the rest of the time whatever sexual activity we've had, we've actually had with other people. What is it you say, Kath: "Never live with your lover?"
>
> *Kathryn:* I think that's good advice.
>
> *Susan:* Do you think of yourselves as lovers?
>
> *Kathryn:* No.
>
> *Margery:* No way. We haven't been in any kind of sexual connection for years. And by

sexual I mean physically, genitally . . . I think the word love we could use, though perhaps not lovers. Love in the broadest and deepest sense. Kath is not only the light of my life but the scourge of my life sometimes. So I think that's real love! I don't know what she thinks about me; I think she loves me in her fashion." (Kathryn is nodding.)

Later,

Kathryn: I think we would agree this is one of the main characteristics of our relationship: that we are absolute opposites in most things.
Margery: Totally incompatible, really.

Although Margery and Kathryn may like to emphasize their differences, as we know, they say they're "opposites in most things":

Susan: You said when we started out, how really, really different you are. Now this capacity to share each other with other people strikes me as a very important similarity.
Margery: That's true; I never thought about it that way.

Margery and Kathryn retired and moved to Northern Wisconsin, where they live in a large comfortable cabin on several remote acres. They are isolated geographically and socially and are more "together" now than they've ever been in their lives:

> *Kathryn:* My retirement and moving here have meant we had to be confined to each other a big part of the time. I'm sure we've never had this experience, and I expect very few people have the experience of being so totally isolated with each other for such long periods of time as we do here.

This isolation together is a Close Couple's idea of heaven; this Separate Couple's idea of . . . well, if not hell, certainly something to be newly negotiated.

The Idea of Difference

There are two ways that the idea of difference needs to be understood. Both difficult, both necessary.

One is that each of us is different from her partner. The women in this study have many ways of giving us this message: "Do not expect someone else to be you;" "Realize that everyone has her own identity;" "We must have the ability to 'cut each other slack,' to allow for each other's differences."

No matter how hard she may try, no matter how earnestly you may coach her, your partner will always fail: she will never be you. This realization can be traumatic. She is profoundly separate from you, profoundly different.

Even your experiences of the relationship are not the same. You may think you are living as part of the same couple, but you're not. Or you are, but only in an approximate fashion. My partner says ours is the easiest relationship she's ever been in; I say, no, for me it's the hardest. For a long time we argued about who was right. It took us several years to realize we're not in the same relationship; she is living with me, one experience; and I am living with her, a very different experience.

I think many of us want the support that is implied by our partner's being the same as us: liking the same things, dressing the same way, having had the same experiences, interpreting reality the same, coming to the same conclusions. Close couples work for and achieve this feeling of sameness and thrive on it; they minimize their differences and emphasize their similarities. Separate couples are more aware of their differences and accentuate them, creating a clear space for themselves as individuals within the relationship.

Many of us are somewhere in between, alternating between close and separate, feeling merged, then distant. Sometimes getting it just right . . . for a while. This feeling of balance, of the right degree of closeness, the right amount of distance, varies for each couple. Developing your own unique blend is the key.

The other thing we need to understand about differences has to do with our lesbian culture. If, as a lesbian, I am already so different from the larger, heterosexual culture, how can I tolerate more difference yet, difference within my own group, the group upon whom I am so dependent for acknowledgement, support and approval? How can I stand the idea that lesbians are as diverse as we are different from the larger culture? Since we're talking here about lesbian couples, do I really have to acknowledge, understand, and appreciate all those different kinds of lesbian couples: unequal couples, butch-femme couples, merged couples, lesbian couples with children, interracial couples, WASP couples, monogamous couples, non-sexual couples? Does just *anybody* get to be a long-term lesbian couple?

By now you know, the answer is Yes. In this book we're meeting all manner of couples: couples just like you, and couples so different from you, you did not imagine they existed (at least I hope I've found some like that for you). The challenge for us is to respect them all, for their struggle, and for their success. We don't have to be like them; we just have to value them. That's what appreciating our diversity means.

A Note about Butch-Femme Couples

A popular myth is that the typical long-term couple is a butch-femme couple, one partner being masculine, the other feminine, and the two dividing up identities and tasks accordingly.

I found this not to be the case. Among the thirty-four couples I interviewed (The questionnaires did not contain any material relevant to butch-femme distinctions.), the longest couple (fifty-two years) is modeled on a butch-femme pattern. The other 33 couples did not appear to be differentiated into butch-femme roles.

Butch-femme roles appear to characterize a particular period in our lesbian history rather than being a necessary arrangement for the longevity of a couple. In fact most couples, and especially those which have formed since the beginning of the modern feminist movement, explicitly reject these roles.

Particular Differences: Income

Our most significant commonality as lesbian couples is that we are both women. The second common feature is that we all — or nearly all — work. Lillian Faderman, in *Surpassing the Love of Men,* her fascinating study of women's romantic friendships from the Renaissance to the present, believes that the most significant difference between then and now is our 20th Century opportunity to work. Faderman believes that, thanks to the financial independence being able to work brings, "Now a woman can hope to carry on a love relationship with another woman for life. It can become her primary relationship, as it seldom could have with romantic friends of the past for economic reasons if no other." Work is important because it allows us to live independent of men and to live as lesbians.

Most of the lesbians in long-term couples work fulltime or have worked in the past and are now retired. Most are highly satisfied with their jobs. Seventy-eight percent said they were very satisfied, and 25 percent said they were extremely satisfied. Only 7.1 percent were quite dissatisfied.

Thanks to high levels of education and consistent work lives, many enjoy comfortable incomes. But while nearly everyone works, or did before they retired, and most are financially secure, not everyone makes the same amount of money. In fact, the

TABLE 3.4 COMPARING INCOME WITHIN COUPLES

Income differences	Number of couples	Percent of couples
Difference of less than $10,000	57	53.3
Diff = $10,000–$20,000	22	20.6
Diff = $20,001–$35,000	18	16.8
Diff = $35,001 or more	10	9.3
Total	107*	100.0

*Number of women who responded to this question.

partners in a couple may differ dramatically in their incomes. How do these couples cope with such differences? Table 3.4 shows the range of income differences within the couples.

Many couples with very large income discrepancies between them report no problems dealing with this difference:

— a seventeen-year couple. One woman makes $75,000, the other $30,000:

"I believe we are unique; we don't fight about money. We have always had our money together and shared expenses equally. We have taken turns going to school, who made more money, etc. We negotiate all large purchases."

— a thirteen-year couple. One woman makes $26,000, the other $3,000:

The poorer partner says, "My lover pays all our bills. My money goes for special things like trips or emergencies."

But others report probelms, most related to the feelings of inequality:

— a twelve-year couple. One woman makes $31,000, the other $10,000. This is in response to a question about equality: "I feel it is important for us to be equals. Initially in our relationship my partner was not working and was very non-assertive and dependent on me. She has grown a great deal in independence and assertiveness. I am more comfortable with this. I like having a partner who is my equal in most matters. When she was not working, and I was her whole world, I felt uncomfortable, like I was responsible for her total happiness. It was a big responsibility."

A more typical response seems to be a practical handling of this potentially awkward situation:

— a nineteen-year couple. Incomes of $45,000 and $25,000. In response to the question about equality, the woman who makes $25,000 says, "Even though we do almost everything together, I feel we are individuals, and equal. Two souls united as one. The importance of equality depends on equal what: Our jobs are not equal in pay, and that seems to be okay. We share equally in our money. We share equally in our jobs at home, almost."

Reviewing the questionnaires and thinking about the interviews, the impression I have is that work and money are important to these couples, but they seem to approach such potentially explosive issues with considerable equanimity. They are worried if they don't have enough money, and they may feel uneasy if they aren't contributing equally, but for these lesbians, money issues do not seem overloaded with powerful emotional symbolism.

Particular Differences: Class

Class differences are another matter. When the partners in a couple have class differences, these differences matter, much more than income disparities. The reason, I think, is because class identification has to do with more than money. It involves beliefs and values, work and play habits, standards of right and wrong. Class has to do with family, with where you came from, with loyalty to how your parents did things. Have you noticed what fights we can have that hinge on how our mothers kept the house we grew up in; or how they made meat loaf; or *if* they made meat loaf?

Mary Pat and Beryl, an eighteen-year couple, share a working class background they think is important to their relationship:

> *Mary Pat:* I just think Beryl and I basically have very similar values.
> *Susan:* What's an example of what you mean by values?

Mary Pat: Well, we're both raised working class. She was raised on a farm, and I was raised in the city, but blue collar. This means if you want something, you work for it, it's not given to you. And that you're respectful of other people. Just sort of the basics. We were taught the same things even if we don't always act them out.

Beryl: Basic manners, saying please and thank you.

Mary Pat: We're basically quite conservative, in that sense.

Beryl: I think those values are important no matter what happens and no matter how sophisticated our society likes to think it is or how yuppie. It still comes down to basics. It's about treating people halfway decent.

When class background is shared, as it is for many of the couples, no problems arise because the identification is so basic that it scarcely bears mentioning; we don't question our most fundamental assumptions.

When there's a difference, it can have a significant impact. Margery and Kathryn, the twenty-four-year separate couple you met earlier, have a wide class difference:

Susan: So you two come from real different families.

Kathryn: And a different social class.

Margery: Very different. The meanest thing Kathryn can say to me is "Rich city kid."

She grew up with a single parent. Her
father died, and her mother had to work
outside the home. I used to say I was lower
class in Ardmore, outside Philadelphia
where I grew up, because our maid didn't
live in. We were literally looked down on.
And Kathryn would say, "My mother *was*
the maid!"

Susan: But the class difference hasn't made
money a big issue?

Margery: No. She has more money than I
have, much more.

Kathryn: I think being impoverished in
childhood is what accounted for my being
very penurious and therefore massing up
some resources.

Margery: Thanks to the money Kathryn's made
and saved, I'm allowed to live in the
manner to which I am accustomed.

In this couple, Kathryn's working class
background has made the security of her own money
very important to her. By contrast, Margery's upper
middle class childhood allows her to assume she will
be taken care of — in this case, ironically, by
Kathryn. Their differences of class intersect to form a
significant area of interdependence.

Particular Differences: Race/Culture

Mattie and Rena, a twelve-year interracial couple,
believe their class differences create difficulties as
often as their racial and cultural differences.

113

Susan: Tell me about your attitudes toward the fact that you're different races: what's good about it? what's bad about it? what's changed about it over the years . . .?

Mattie (Black and middle class): Sometimes the issue crops up in the damnedest ways. Real unexpected. Because not only are we different races, but we're different classes. And the way I was raised was expectations, and . . .

Rena (Polish and working class): . . . no chuck steak.

Mattie: My family's rules and expectations were much different from the rules and expectations she was raised with. Sometimes they're the same, and they blend real nice, like we're both committed to family. But other times we're like screaming at each other. Once we get down to it, it's just a whole cultural thing.

Rena: It's more apt to be a class thing than a race thing.

Mattie More apt to be a class thing. Sometimes it's both, and I can't always separate it out. I mean, there are some things that well-brought-up black middle class girls do. And I can't get away from them all the time. Some of the things are so ingrained in me, I can't always let them go; they're just part of who I am.

Rena: Like always being polite when it's totally tedious and whoever is visiting just needs to be asked to go away.

Later,

Mattie: The race thing can be important, though. Like I refuse to always go places where there's no black people. I don't care how hungry I am, if a place looks redneck, I'm not goin' in there to eat.

Rena: When we first got together, I don't think I was tuned in to the vibes that bothered Mattie. I mean, I lived with so many rednecks! My experience with most rednecks is that they're like my father. They have this big political bullshit, but person-to-person they're okay, you know. So I had to learn how it was that Mattie could be uncomfortable.

Mattie: Well, tell her about our first date. Where did you take me?

Rena: Oh God. Don't tell her. I'll be embarrassed.

Mattie: Where did you take me?

Rena: I took her to "Gone with the Wind." I had never seen "Gone with the Wind" with those eyes — through a black person's eyes — before!

Deborah and Kathy have been together thirteen years, and their differences cut a lot of ways. Deborah is an upper middle class Jewish Easterner. Kathy is poor, working class, Protestant, and Midwestern.

Kathy: For me there's always been a thing about money and about saving and about

115

paying your way, and real strong stuff about getting an education. Except that when you go to college as a poor kid you never really feel like you belong there; you feel like pretty soon somebody is going to find you out, that you're not smart enough.

Deborah: Because I was raised upper middle class, I always felt a sense of security and optimism about things working out; the world felt full of opportunity.

Kathy: We had differences about what you wear, and how you talk, and how much you worry about money . . . lots of things. But we didn't know what they were. We would just be kind of annoyed with each other. When we finally identified what these issues were, it helped a lot. Now we can say: "Oh, that's just class stuff!

Susan: It's funny how that helps, isn't it? Just naming something, knowing the origins of it. For one thing, it depersonalizes it . . . So what would be a practical example of a class issue between you?

Deborah: Some of the most dramatic stuff has to do with visiting our families. When my father and his second wife had their tenth anniversary, they decided the whole family should have a vacation together. And guess where it was? The Bahamas.

Kathy: My dad's idea of great entertainment is watching Home Box Office on TV.

Particular Differences: Age

More than half the women are within five years of their partner in age. But 16 percent of the couples are separated by eleven years or more. Table 3.5 gives the breakdown.

Age differences make more of a difference at the beginning and at the end of our individual and couple lives. If couples first get together when the women are relatively young, a large age difference can make the older feel she's exploiting the younger, or at least her friends can accuse her of that:

Beryl: I left my relationship of four years abruptly and was ostracized by my friends for going out with someone so young. (I was 24 and my partner was 16.) My friends were angry, her friends were angry, so we

TABLE 3.5 AGE DIFFERENCES WITHIN COUPLES

Age discrepancy	Number of couples	Percent of couples
Five years age difference or less	59	54.6
6 to 10 years	32	29.6
11 to 15 years	14	13.0
16 to 20 years	3	2.8
Total	108	100.0

117

bonded together quite quickly and strongly. (18-year couple)

Some relationships start out with age differences that are ignored by the couple. Later, though, the age difference may parallel and thus symbolize and reinforce a power difference that one of the partners comes to resent:

> *Sue:* Melanie is fourteen years older than I, and I was twenty-two years old when we got together, sort of another kid to her, since she already had three kids. When I got to be thirty (this would be eight years into their twelve-year relationship), I didn't like being treated like a kid any more, and this was a big problem. We are still working on this, and it's getting better. (age 34, 12-year couple)

Another woman describes her experience:

> *Gladyce:* My partner is eight years older than me. I felt soon after we moved in together that she wanted to give her opinion whether I asked for it or not. Control over me was necessary. If I disagreed with her, we argued. Some call it control, and others trying to be "butch."
>
> I soon decided she loved me in her way, and I wouldn't disagree. However, this didn't solve the problem. After eighteen years, I began to rebel!
>
> We consulted a psychologist and

118

continued seeing her for two years. We had
our trials and tribulations, but we have
greatly improved things. Now our
relationship is stronger than ever! Thank
God for qualified, caring counselors." (age
52, a 20-year couple)

At the end of our life spans, age differences begin
to make a tragic difference:

Mary: My only sorrow is that since there is a
sixteen year difference in our ages, our
relationship won't go on forever. I cannot
contemplate living without Nancy or with
someone else. I would only wish that
everyone could experience a relationship
like this. It's better after twenty years than
it was at the beginning! (age 42, 20-year
couple)

I believe that age difference is not so significant
in itself, except at the end of our lives. What is
important is when a disparity of ages parallels a
disparity of power. Here is a woman expressing how
an age difference paralleled other areas of inequality
she and her partner perceived in their relationship,
and how this inequality has worked itself out over
time:

Rae: I'm seven years older and was an
established professional when we met. We
both worked from the beginning to have
this professional-monetary disparity NOT be
an issue. Now we are professionally on a

par and most of the differences due to age and my being established are gone. Being equal partners, to the extent that has been possible, has been important. Having joint accounts and possessions (the house) in common, has greatly fostered the feeling of equality. (age 45, a 16-year couple)

Equality

A feeling of equality is key in lesbian relationships:

"Equality is very important to me. I'm not just a partner. I am equal to her and she to me. If we are not equal, we have nothing together." (Virginia, age 51, 23-year couple)

Need I say more? How I phrased the question was: "Some women find that being in an equal relationship with their partner is very important to them. Others do not feel this way. What importance do you feel issues around equality have had for your relationship?"

"Enormous. The equality issue is probably the one that kept me from marrying heterosexually." (Lillian, age 60, 31-year couple)

This is a point many women make about what is to them a principal drawback of heterosexual relationships; they're innately unequal.

"I feel that equality is a cornerstone of a good relationship. I think that inequality is one of the biggest strikes against heterosexual marriage. We were all raised in a patriarchy, and whether we subscribe to the philosophy or not, we all know what the roles are. I think it is nearly impossible for a young man and woman to get together and make it work." (Annie, age 44, 12-year couple)

Some couples struggle with the issue:

"Equality has been a major issue in our relationship. Initially my partner had much more "power" in the relationship. We've worked hard to equalize the power, and at this point I believe we've achieved it." (Sarah, age 34, 10-year couple)

For others, equality comes easily:

"Equality is not much of an issue for us. We both are very independent and assume that we will share decisions-responsibilities equally." (Fran, age 36, 11-year couple)

Notice that Sarah is talking about "power" and Fran is talking about "sharing decisions and responsibilities." Equality, besides being important, is defined differently by different couples.

"Equality is very important, because her ideas and opinions are just as valid as mine."

"Equality is of major importance. I value my own growth as a person as much as I value my relationship. Therefore, I need a relationship that allows respect, responsibility, and acknowledgement, which only occurs in an equal atmosphere."

"Because we became involved at the beginning of the women's movement, equality was always important as a contrast to our experiences with men. I still believe that even though everyone has different skills and contributes differently to the relationship, there must be equal respect and power in the relationship — as well as equal recognition for each other's contributions."

"Equality is extremely important. When one of us feels less recognition, input in decisions, independence, etc., there is always some friction and generally open conflict."

Although different couples discuss equality in different terms, some themes emerge: equality has to do with power, decision-making, respect, recognition, and acknowledgement. Emma sums it up:

"We don't have to have equal money, or do equal things. We need to feel we have equal value, power, and rights in the relationship." (15-year couple)

All the women agree that not everyone's skills, interests, preferences or earning power are the same and therefore equal. We're not identical creatures. What is important, though, and what constitutes real equality, is valuing equally what each partner contributes: "As long as no chore is seen as useless or any feeling irrelevant."

Another insight these couples have is a recognition that a sense of equality is achieved over time. In fact, sometimes equality itself can only be realized over time.

"Equality is — was certainly a biggie for us in the beginning. Everything had to be equal, from reciprocal backrubs, to money, to the last piece of cake. However, that got old when we realized how much energy it took to keep tabs. Each of us now knows that we will get what we need from this relationship when we need it." (Mattie, 12-year couple)

"I used to believe that we, as partners, should equally share expenses, chores, and should do all things together. But over the years I have come to accept that we each have strengths and weaknesses at different — and sometimes the same — times, and we must learn to draw strengths from each other when weak, and be willing to share when strong." (Edith, age 39, 15-year couple)

"Equal does not necessarily mean fifty-fifty all the time. It can be sixty-forty or forty-sixty, at times eighty-twenty or twenty-eighty. However, it should average out to fifty percent each. If you have trust. . . ." (Joanne, age 68, 18-year couple)

With experience in our long-term relationship we can come to trust that what we give today will be returned to us tomorrow . . . even if tomorrow is a long time coming. Besides, we need to keep a little perspective and not overvalue what we think we're giving. A woman in a twenty-year couple offers some sobering advice: "Give what you consider eighty to ninety percent in a relationship, and you're probably giving your fifty percent!"

Inequality/Power Differences

I asked, "In general, who has more say about important decisions affecting your relationship, you or your partner?" and "In general, who would you say has more power or influence in the relationship, you or your partner?" A full 90.3 percent (195 women) feel they both have equal say. In a discussion of inequality, however, we need to pay attention to those at the extremes of the distribution. Six women feel they have more say than their partners, and fifteen say their partners have more than they do. This means the woman with less power is more likely to recognize the imbalance than the person with more power.

This is true for Pat and Anna, the fifty-two-year couple. Anna says Pat has more say over important decisions (R = 8). Pat says they're equal (R = 5). The same pattern between these two women holds true for the next question, the one about who has more power or influence. Anna says Pat does (R = 7). Pat says they both do. Anna, by the way, in answer to another question: "Who do you think *should* have the final say about important decisions. . . ?" says that Pat should (R = 7).

(The scale runs from, 1 = I have much more say, to 9 = She has much more say. Specific responses are reported as follows: R = 8 means Anna's response was 8 on the 1 to 9 scale, that is, she feels Pat has much more say. This reporting style is used throughout the book.)

When asked about power and influence, again a majority, though this time not as large (123 women, 56.9 percent), feel they and their partner share power and influence equally in the relationship. Four-fifths of the group choose the middle three responses, 4, 5, and 6, indicating perceptions of fairly equal power and influence. Some women, however, perceive inequalities, even extreme inequalities. Fourteen are willing to say they have considerably more power or influence than their partners. In fact, two women are willing to claim all the power (R = 1). Twenty-seven women feel their partner has considerably more power than them, with three feeling she has all the power (R = 9).

Here's a couple, together thirteen years, where one partner feels the other has more say (R = 7) and slightly more power (R = 6). Carol says:

"Equality has pretty much importance. We feel pretty equal. But she has more say in house-related issues (which is fine with me)."

Her partner Cora, who admits to slightly more say

125

(R = 4) but equal power (R = 5), elaborates with honesty and detail:

"This is sticky. Although I hate to admit to 'roles' (because I consider myself to be a feminine 'butch'), I guess we do play roles to a certain extent. She confesses to book smarts but no common sense, thus I have the privilege (and responsibility) of making most decisions regarding the house. I think she will agree, however, that neither tries to 'rule' over the house. We try to come to mutual agreement on things. I think it has made it easier that she doesn't like to make house and yard decisions.

I must confess that lately I have felt like her mother, trying to get her to do her part, and that's no good." (This woman, at 49, is ten years older than her partner.)

Here's another relatively unequal situation, the women together eleven years:

"We both want things to be more equal. Sometimes I am spoiled and just let things go on as they are. If she will do all for me (like a wife), I take. I'm more stressed and less efficient given the same circumstances, so she 'does,' while I 'reflect.'" (age 39)

Her partner, age 41:

"I don't mind inequality, as long as we continue to love each other."

126

Some women suggest that power imbalances for lesbian couples are matters of personality rather than externals, like age or income: "In every relationship there are stronger and weaker personalities. That's inevitable." I'm not sure I would say "stronger" and "weaker" — maybe more and less controlling, more and less shy or afraid, more and less verbal — but I think they may be right, that personalities play a big part. Here's a woman, in an eighteen-year relationship, responding to the question about their biggest source of problems:

"Our biggest problem is me being too powerful, she feeling powerless. Me wanting to not have that happen, she anticipating it happening again. Each of us reacting and overreacting to the continued cycle."

Lesbians do have problems with equality,

"Equality has been important for issues around trust: being taken advantage of was a fear of both of ours. Some of our earlier conflicts (who works more, brings home money, does most chores, etc.) were issues relating to trust." (age 34, a 12-year couple)

but the problems reflect the fact that we place such a high value on achieving a feeling of equality, a feeling that the contributions each of us make to the relationship are valued equally.

"I feel equality issues have been focal throughout much of our time together. We have struggled with identity and its loss; dependence versus independence; control, i.e., who's the boss here? Eventually we are coming to understand that equality is not so much a balancing of scales as it is a sense of fairness and justice, given our individual differences." (age 41, 15-year couple)

STORY 4:

MAUDE (age 78) & AGNES (age 75):
41 years together

Maude and Agnes have retired to the property they bought years ago in a small resort community on Cape Cod. They live on a large, slightly overgrown lot with trees and flower beds and lots of birds. Their house has an attractive helter-skelter feel to it; everybody who has owned it has added a room here or there. They live — in the summer anyway, when I visited them — on the large screened-in porch on the front of the house, where they watch the passing scene. Everything is in a state of lived-in mussiness.

They are comfortable financially, but not wealthy. Their assets are their property.

This couple is politically liberal. Feminism is central to their personal and political identities, and they are eloquent about their feminist principles. Yet they are quite conservative when it comes to identifying as lesbians. They are closeted from their best friends (also a long-term lesbian couple) in the sense that the four of them never discuss the fact that they are all lesbians. This despite the fact that one of the friends is an ex-lover of Agnes's. They are closeted from other friends and acquaintances; there are very few people with whom they are open.

We talked about gay rights parades and other forms of publicly acknowledging one's lesbianism, but such displays they feel would violate their privacy:

> *Agnes:* I could never wear a sign and go out and march and stuff like that, basically because I still feel that our personal life is intensely private and personal. We have a greater sense of privacy, I think, than many younger people.
> *Susan:* And marching about lesbian rights would violate that sense of privacy?
> *Agnes:* Yes. It just is repugnant.
> *Maude:* We were raised in an age of taboos. It's hard to get away from taboos.

These same women, with their inbred sense of privacy and fairly high degree of concealment, have nonetheless made major contributions to the lesbian community. (How so, they of course don't want me to say.)

Susan: But over the years you have. . . .

Maude: Yes, and Agnes went along with me; I couldn't have done it by myself. It was our joint money that did it, not mine. And in the early days, we both had to do much of the day-to-day work.

One time a woman who was going to distribute literature for us couldn't come, so I suggested I go and mind the booth. Well, I don't think Agnes liked that. She did drive me there, and we both set up the booth. But then she went and stood on the other side of the street! She didn't want to be seen with me.

Agnes: You see, I didn't identify myself with a name, a category, here. I dislike anybody else putting me in that category, too. (To Maude) You want to find some words for me here?

Maude: I know how you feel about it. I have always felt I had better armor against attacks from outside, or potential ones, were we more open. Agnes is more sensitive to that sort of thing.

Maude and Agnes met over forty years ago in Boston. Maude: "I looked out of my office window and saw her across the street. That was it." Agnes was already involved with a woman, but this was Maude's first experience of falling in love since a heartbreak of twenty years earlier:

Maude: I had a very bad crush on somebody when I was young, but that had come to nothing; she ended up a nun. So that gave me a very dark view of things, a very biased view of human relationships; I didn't want any, you see. By the time I met Agnes I was 38.

Agnes was living life as a reluctant bisexual; a life she found very unsatisfying: "I was disgusted with myself. I was really surprised that Maude was interested in me." Maude: "Well, you were a pearl as far as I was concerned. I really did feel that. I thought you'd been led astray." Maude wanted Agnes to stop seeing other lovers, and to be committed and faithful to her alone:

Maude: My point of view was not the point of view that she had become accustomed to.

Susan: Did you discuss being faithful right at the beginning? Was that explicitly talked about?

Maude: Oh yes. If Agnes didn't want that, then we wouldn't have gone together. It would not have changed my feeling for her, but our relationship would not have gone forward. Because I think a true relationship has to have commitment. And when I say commitment, I mean commitment. I mean you put in everything.

Susan: Do you think, Agnes, you were looking for somebody to be committed to?

Agnes: I don't think so.

Susan: Then what was attractive about Maude to you?

Agnes: Well, she obviously thought quite a lot of me.

Agnes had been living with an aunt for fourteen years, since she was twenty. Agnes invited Maude to rent a room in her aunt's house, and thus they became a couple. The relationship between Maude and Agnes was difficult because of the presence of Agnes's aunt, a woman who mothered Agnes and toward whom Agnes felt great love and loyalty.

Maude: The aunt was lucky to have Agnes.
Agnes: I was lucky to have her.

Agnes explains more about the situation,

Agnes: My aunt's parents had just died, and she needed someone to stay with her. Well, it ended up I was with her forty-some years! I simply could not leave my aunt. She had given me a home and her love and attention and contemplated that I would live with her permanently.

The relationship among the three was an emotional triangle.

Maude: Agnes viewed her aunt as a child would a mother, whereas I think her aunt — I'm sure she didn't realize this entirely — her aunt's feelings toward her were those of a lover.

Susan: Oh, do you think so?
Maude: Oh, yes.
Agnes: Yes, I think so. Yes, I do.

Agnes's aunt lived to be ninety-one, and Agnes and Maude lived as a couple — a very discreet couple — with her for twenty-eight years. Even with the aunt's presence they were able to be close sexually.

Susan: So you each had your own room?
Maude: (Chuckles) Theoretically I did!

It's been thirteen years since Agnes's aunt died and they have been able to be alone. Agnes: "We're home free now."
This couple has maintained sex in their relationship throughout their forty-one years together. When I told them that many couples together for a very long time are no longer sexual, they were surprised.

Maude: Really? I find that rather strange.
Agnes: Have they grown apart, or. . . .
Susan: No, they still feel affectionate, hug and kiss, sleep in the same bed, but they're not genitally sexual any more. They explain away their sexual urge. They say, for instance, "Well, we hit menopause."
Agnes: Why, that's ridiculous!
Maude: That is.
Agnes: What difference does that make?
Susan: Well, they think it's hormones, that without those hormones, they don't feel as sexual.

Agnes: Well, it's all a matter of mind! If you're just too bored with each other to create any sort of imaginative stimulus, I can see where sex would die out.

Maude: Well, we certainly stimulate each other.

They talk for a while about friends they know who are aging, and speculate about how sexual they may be. But their attention comes back to themselves.

Agnes: Actually, I don't see any difference in myself except that when I realize I'm seventy-five, I'm appalled. My mother was dead when she was seventy-five.

Maude: It's true that physical disabilities do get in the way. So that you can't . . . you don't . . . (she searches for a sufficiently genteel way to say this . . . and finds it) . . . you're not as limber as when you were younger. But that has nothing to do with what you would like to do or, you know. . . .

Susan: Do you intentionally do things with each other to be romantic? Is it something you're conscious of wanting to preserve in your relationship?

Maude: We never have done that, have we? We've not done things to feel romantic. That was one thing you used to tell me about your other friends, Agnes. They'd go in for all kinds of what I thought were very odd, official things, like gazing at the moon. Which I always thought was a lot of nonsense.

Susan: So it isn't as if you're wooing each other all the time?

Maude: No, that would be very tiresome, I would think. No, I just want to be as close to her as I always have been. Physically as close to her, and sex is part of it. I think that maybe some people begin to lose that feeling for contact. Would you suppose that's it?

Susan: It seems that they still have contact. It would be like, you know, sitting, watching TV, holding hands.

Agnes: Well, we only look at the news.

A bit later,

Susan: Do you think the fact that you are sexual makes your relationship different than it would be if you weren't being sexual together?

Maude: I think so. I think the importance of sex — outside of the physical gratification — the importance is that it's the ultimate contact. If you have a very close relationship, sex is that one closest link.

Agnes: I think I'm more affectionate generally.

Maude: By nature, yes. She's more gregarious and tends to be more openly affectionate. Though I think from living with her I've become a little more so . . . People have different physical natures, I suppose. It's hard to make a rule. There are some people who don't seem to like physical contact.

Susan: Or passionate contact. The difference

seems to be between passion and not. All the couples like quite a bit of physical contact, in a huggy-kissy kind of way. But when it gets to something more passionate than that, that's something that's dropped out of many couples' lives together.

Maude: Well, it hasn't with us; I can assure you.

The relationship between Maude and Agnes does not seem equal. Maude is a very controlling person. I was struck by her dominance and Agnes's submissiveness, but they are also interdependent. They are interdependent intellectually. Their relationship is verbal and interactive; they talk about ideas:

> *Agnes:* I must admit as I get older I'm somewhat prejudiced in certain things, and I think we tend to keep each other a little bit broad-minded. If we disagree with each other, we say so; it keeps you from becoming bigoted and narrow-minded. You get jolted all the time so that your mind is active and. . . .
>
> *Maude:* Your feelings are active, not atrophied in any way.

Agnes depends on Maude for direction and a sense of self-esteem: "Maude has a much better presence than I do. I rely on her to explain me. If I get mad enough, I'll explain myself; I don't have any difficulty at all then!"

Maude depends on Agnes for much of the practical

137

work of living. Agnes cooks and runs errands. Agnes is the more sociable of the two, and Maude recognizes that without her influence, she would have lived a much more isolated life. She depends on Agnes to negotiate between her and the outside world: "I'll very often let Agnes deal with people about things."

They finish sentences for each other (although Maude finishes Agnes's much more often than vice versa):

> *Agnes:* We don't . . . one of us doesn't really
> like to do something. . . .
> *Maude:* . . . that excludes the other.

Even though Maude is a dominant person, we can't forget that she adapted herself to the many uncomfortable years with Agnes's aunt. Nonetheless, I think it's clear that Maude's personality has shaped the way the relationship and their lives have gone. I think Agnes would not object. I think, in fact, she's grateful. Though sometimes rebellion surfaces: "She makes me have certain things for my health; it's always for my benefit. Every once in a while, I don't want something for my benefit."

It is a sad truth that no couple can be together forever; any permanent couple is eventually parted by death. At one point in the interview Maude and Agnes had this exchange. I had asked what each liked best about being in a long relationship:

> *Maude:* I find that hard to answer, because I
> can't imagine not being in one with Agnes.
> Not just any long relationship, but being
> without Agnes. Of course this is going to

pose a problem one of these days, no doubt; I'm older than you are.

Agnes: It's one of my nightmares now.

Susan: What is?

Agnes: Well, we're not going to live forever; one of us is going to go first. So Maude has said on occasion that she hopes it's me, so I won't have to. . . .

Maude: I really do hope that I outlive you. I wouldn't like to leave you behind. But . . . this upsets me.

Susan: You feel as if you'd be able to carry on more easily than Agnes would?

Maude: Well, yes and no. I don't know. I would manage somehow, I suppose, as long as I live. But she's so vulnerable . . . she's very sensitive to human relationships and to loss. Having seen her through quite a number of losses, I wouldn't like to think that she's going to be left to handle this one alone. (Agnes is crying and leaves for a while.)

While she was gone I asked Maude again what she liked about their long relationship.

Susan: If it doesn't make sense to talk about long relationships in general, tell me what you've liked best about this relationship with Agnes.

Maude: It's like having another self. You're not alone even in your thoughts.

Chapter 4
Sexuality

Being Friends with Our Partners

All of our relationships grow and change, but most of them remain "just friends." A very few relationships, maybe only one, combine being friends with being lovers. That is the combination the lesbians in long-term couples think is crucially important.

Remember the question about the three most

significant factors that explain why a couple stayed together? Love was the factor overwhelmingly chosen as most significant. Common values/goals/interests was second. Commitment was third. And tied with commitment as the third most significant factor was friendship:

"This partner is my best friend, I rely on her support." (Nancy, age 37, 12-year couple)

"We like each other. We truly enjoy each other's company, amaze each other, surprise and delight each other." (Suzanne, age 39, 10-year couple)

When asked, "What do you think forms the heart of a successful relationship?", these women say:

"Trust. Being able to talk to each other in all things. Understanding one another's feelings. Lots of love from the heart, and not just the mouth. And being a good friend as well as a lover." (Norma, age 67, a 32-year couple)

"Compatibility. Similar likes in people and other interests. Becoming good friends as well as lovers. Mutual respect. Integrity and trust. I would emphasize trust." (Julia, age 64, 33-year couple)

When asked, "What advice do you have for other women who want to stay together?", these lesbians say,

"Put your relationship first; Believe it will last; spend time together; talk; be friends as well as lovers." (Judith, age 37, 13-year couple)

"Make sure you can be friends before you're lovers. Treat your partner as you want to be treated. Always talk things out together." (Corinne, age 63, 23-year couple)

Notice several themes implicit in these quotes. The idea of trust is linked with the importance of friendship: "My advice is to find someone where there is mutual love and trust, wanting the best for each other." I can't think of a better definition of friendship than that: wanting the best for each other. Nor can I think of a better reason to trust your partner than a belief that she wants the best for you.

Some of the comments also suggest that one make friends with a prospective partner before passion intervenes. These women know this is a tall order: "Try to make the time to be friends first and then lovers." They, like all of us, know that that early period when we are falling in love and being most sexual is an impossible time to judge how you and your partner will fare over time.

I have joked with friends — but I think it's true — that during the early months of an infatuation, we almost completely misrepresent ourselves to our new love. Everything about us is unusual; nothing is typical. Our priorities are totally reordered; we care about nothing but being with our loved one. We lose weight; our appetites have only one focus. We have heightened energy; we are tireless. We want to make love all the time; we never say no. We are experimental and risk-taking; we live life on the edge.

It isn't until we calm down a few weeks, months, or years later that our true, sober selves emerge. It turns out we care about our work, we have a problem with food, we are tired at night, we have to be in the mood, we value security. How was our partner to know any of this ahead of time? Falling passionately in love is about bonding; it is not about accurate self disclosure.

The suggestion that we be friends first is motivated by the recognition that, over the long haul, passion will calm. Whether we like our partner will become paramount. We were terribly attracted to her . . . we wanted her . . . our souls were joined . . . but do we like her? Being friends first suggests that, down the line, the answer to this crucial question will be "yes." "At the very root of things, like the other person more than anyone else you know." (Vanessa, age 35, 12-year couple)

Identifying as Lesbian/Gay

How do the women in long-term lesbian couples define their own sexual orientation? I asked: "Do you and your partner consider yourselves a lesbian couple, or a gay couple, or do you identify simply as two women living together in a primary relationship, or how do you describe your relationship to yourselves?"

The great majority (71 percent) of the women in this study identify themselves as being part of a lesbian couple. Table 4.1 gives the complete breakdown.

144

TABLE 4.1 COUPLE IDENTIFICATION

Identification as . . .	Number of women	Percent of women
Lesbian couple	150	71.1
Gay couple	21	10.0
Two women living together in primary relationship	24	11.4
Permanently committed couple	2	0.9
Married couple	4	1.9
Other	10	4.7
Total	211*	100.0

*Number of women who responded to this question.

We already know from the introduction that the word lesbian is difficult for some women. Others, however, are clearly more than comfortable with both the word and the identity:

When asked about race/nationality/ethnic identity, Jill answered: "Race: White/Caucasian; Ethnic Identity: Lesbian." And when asked whether being a lesbian was a conscious choice, Barbara responded: "It's an honor and a privilege."

Not everyone, however, is so sure about the appropriate identity. Here is an example of a very articulate woman who doesn't identify as a lesbian, but who is not hostile to the label either. She is responding to the final question: "Is there anything else you'd like to share with me?"

"Yes. I don't feel gay. I realize by all definitions, of course, I am. It's not a matter of denial; I think I lack a gay identity. To me, it seems like a non-issue. I *have* felt oppressed as a woman . . . denied opportunity, access, respect, but I have never felt oppressed as a lesbian. If anything, my lifestyle increases my power as a woman. I would almost say I crossed over that invisible line as a political choice, but I'd be lying. I did it to love, make love, and be loved, by a woman!" (Jessica, age 44, 12-year couple)

Other women identify as bisexual, although often the claim seems a bit strained. One 71-year-old woman has spent forty-five years in relationships with three women, including twenty-six years with her current partner. She spent four years with a man (not married to him), between the ages of 32 and 36:

"I consider myself a bisexual living in a primary relationship. Obviously a number of our gay friends consider it a lesbian relationship. I don't discuss it with them."

Only one woman in my sample of 216 is currently actively bisexual, and she doesn't claim the identity. More often, what women seem to mean when they identify as bisexual is a feeling of potentiality, rather than a reporting of reality. This position is expressed by Lillian, a 60-year-old woman in a thirty-one-year couple: "I believe that I, like most persons, am bisexual, and I say so whenever possible."

Lillian and her partner Victoria are an interesting blend of sexual identification. Lillian had her first significant relationship — it was with a man — between the ages of 23 and 26. Since then she has been with her female partner for thirty-one years. Her partner, Victoria, 70, identifies closely with being male. Victoria responds to a series of questions about lesbian identity, including whether or not being a lesbian is "beyond one's control" or a matter of "conscious choice."

"This section is hard for me to answer clearly, especially in the context of the current apparent rise in a type of lesbianism which sometimes seems to be almost a matter of conscious choice.

"I don't feel at all typical in this regard. I guess I think each person is a highly complex hormonal/chemical/structural individual, and that my 'structure' from earliest recollection was male-oriented (to myself, I consider ours a husband and wife relationship, though I don't think my partner puts this in these terms as much as my first partner felt it.)

"I confess to not having a deep understanding of the current 'crop' of lesbians who are attracted to each other on a more same sex basis than my make-up encompasses. Is this a generational gap, or do I see this from a different perspective because of a more basic difference in me?"

Perhaps Lillian's identification as bisexual is true in a much more subtle and complex way than we would normally conceive.

Another woman, 39, told me about her early identification as male. Alix and her partner, together for twenty years, were each other's first lesbian

147

lovers, and invented their sexual relationship as they went along.

> *Alix:* I never liked what was female about my body, but Sally did. I had read transsexual stuff and I'd daydream, "Oh, this would be perfect: I'd be the boy or the man. . . ." The whole first year we just ignored the fact that I was female.
>
> *Susan:* What do you mean?
>
> *Alix:* Well, for instance, when we'd make love, I'd keep my clothes on. I'd take my shirt off, but I'd keep my pants on. I can remember real well . . . it would be unthinkable to unzip my pants. Too big a conflict. I don't know about genitalia; I don't think I was ever actually pretending I was male or anything. It was just, my woman's body didn't fit somehow, so I kept it under the clothes.
>
> *Susan:* So what happened with all this?
>
> *Alix:* Just from Sally saying she liked my body, and showing she liked it, then I came to like it. Just fine. I'm glad I just learned to like being a woman.

It is tempting to speculate that women who are uneasy about their identification as lesbians are less likely to enjoy sex with their female partners than are women more comfortable with being lesbians. I didn't find this to be true. Victoria and Lillian have not been sexual for the last nine of their thirty-one years together, but I think the reason has to do with the damage suffered as an aftermath of affairs, not with Victoria's male identification or Lillian's bisexuality. Alix and Sally are intermittently sexual, but Alix's acute identification with being male is twenty years behind her. The reason for the low frequency and dissatisfaction with their sexual relationship again probably has to do with affairs.

Janice, 42, does not identify firmly as a lesbian though she has been in her current relationship for eighteen years. (She substitutes "Being attracted to certain people" for "Being a lesbian" in the questionnaire. She is very closeted. This woman, however, talks far more about the physical nature of her love for her partner than most. She finds the most significant factor in their staying together to be "a very deep and satisfying love (emotional and physical)." She describes the most joyful things about the relationship: "Absolute certainty and mutual trust. Love that is communicated frequently verbally or physically. . . ." She and her partner make love about once a month, and she is extremely satisfied with their sexual relationship. Janice, while hesitant about claiming her lesbianism, is not at all hesitant about claiming its pleasures. Clearly the linkages between sexual identification and sexual attitude and behavior are very complex.

Some women have experienced a fairly consistent lesbian history. Carol-Anne describes her process of gradually adopting a lesbian identity:

"When I was very young (7, 8, 9 years old) I knew that I loved women. When I was a teenager, I never felt attracted to guys, but didn't worry about it much and was not pressured to do so. When I was 17, I fell in

149

love with my partner and knew it was right for me though I had never heard the word lesbian. We lived together as lovers in a committed relationship for many years before I came out to myself and then to others and discovered a lesbian community." (age 31, 14-year couple)

Let's let Carol-Anne have the final word about identifying as a lesbian: "Being gay has brought a richness, an ever-increasing sense of tolerance and compassion, and an ever-growing strength of self-respect to my life."

Sexuality: Attitudes, Behavior

Lesbians in long-term couples are physically very affectionate. They hug and kiss and snuggle; they touch each other a lot. When I asked, "When you look at your relationship as a whole, what would you say are the most joyful things about it? What gives you the most pleasure?" many women talked about the physical pleasure they take in their partners:

"Snuggling every night, we talk, relax, and renew ourselves and our commitment to each other." (Marcia, age 39, 12-year couple)

"I think what gives me the most pleasure is crawling in bed and cuddling up to the warm, soft, voluptuous, sweetly breathing woman that I love." (Shirley, age 33, 12-year couple)

"We like to touch each other." (Fanny, age 60, 22-year couple)

The couples I interviewed typically share the same bedroom and bed. They emphasized how important being physically affectionate is to them. They wanted me to understand that physical contact has remained important to them whether or not genital sex was still present in their relationship. "I still get a kick out of kissin' her and stuff." (Norma, age 67, 32-year couple)

So, there's no question that most long-term lesbian couples are physically close and remain so through the years. But what of sex, what of the genital, orgasmic-type physical contact?

In the Introduction I linked identity as a lesbian with sexual behavior. I defined a lesbian couple as two women, who define themselves as a couple and have been sexual with each other at some time in their relationship. The phrase "at some time in their relationship" recognizes that the amount and duration of sexual expression among lesbian couples may vary. In fact, the way in which lesbians express themselves sexually varies throughout history, throughout the course of their relationships, and throughout their lives.

Lillian Faderman's historical study of romantic friendships between women concludes: "It is likely that most love relationships between women during previous eras, when females were encouraged to force any sexual drive they might have to remain latent, were less physical than they are in our times." And she observes, "It is in our century that love has come to be perceived as a refinement of the sexual impulse." Thus, how sexual we perceive ourselves able to be as women who love women may vary with the historical period in which we find ourselves.

Many woman are also familiar with the way in which their sexual energy ebbs and flows during different stages of their lives. It is common to assume that sexuality is the province of youth, and that interest in sex declines as we age. The research on heterosexual female activity does not unequivocally confirm this assumption. Nonetheless, we all experience times in our lives when we feel less sexual than others. Some of the women in the study report that the times of feeling less sexual correspond with increasing age.

Finally, our sexual expression varies within the context of our relationship. We have all experienced the intense sexuality of the very first few weeks, months, years together. If we have stayed in a relationship long enough, we have also experienced the gradual decline of this intensity, or, if not a decline in intensity, surely a decline in frequency.

I asked the couples about both the frequency and the quality of sexual contact they have experienced in their relationship. The vast majority, 92.3 percent, report that the frequency of sexual contact has decreased since the beginning of their relationship.

Their evaluation of the quality of sexual contact is very different. Table 4.2 shows the responses.

These are some responses to the question about quality:

"During the times when lovemaking is frequent, the quality of sexual contact increases. However, when there are long

TABLE 4.2 CHANGES IN QUALITY OF SEXUAL CONTACT

Since the beginning of our relationship, the quality of our sexual contact has . . .	Number of women	Percent of women
Increased	84	39.8
Decreased	53	25.1
Remained the same	53	25.1
Other	21	10.0
Total	211*	100.0

*Number of women who responded to this question.

periods of little or no sex, the quality decreases." (13-year couple)

"The quality has changed. Generally less lengthy, but perhaps more meaningful now." (18-year couple)

Her partner says,

"The quality has changed. Love-making isn't as intense: less exploration, trying new ways, positions, etc."

When the women discuss frequency of sexual contact, they agree that it varies tremendously, and they often include an evaluation of quality at the same time:

"There have been slow times and fast

times, and they are very good now." (11-year couple)

"Some of the intense passion is less, but the comfortableness has increased. It changes over time. Sex is sometimes more important, sometimes less." (12-year couple)

"Cyclical ups and downs. Seems to be in an 'off' mode now, with stresses and distractions of buying a house. Hope an upcoming vacation makes us more playful and spontaneous." (12-year couple)

I also asked how important these women think their sexual life is to the quality and to the permanence of their relationship. They answered on a nine-point scale, from 1 = Very important to 9 = Not at all important. Tables 4.3 and 4.4 report this information. I have combined responses 1 to 3 into a "Very important" category; 4 to 6, "Moderately important"; and 7 to 9, "Not very important."

These women feel differently about whether sex is

TABLE 4.3 IMPORTANCE OF SEX TO QUALITY OF RELATIONSHIP

Degree of importance	Number of women	Percent of women
Very important	81	38.4
Moderately important	76	36.0
Not very important	54	25.6
Total	211*	100.0

*Number of women who responded to this question.

TABLE 4.4 IMPORTANCE OF SEX TO PERMANENCE OF RELATIONSHIP

Degree of importance	Number of women	Percent of women
Very important	66	31.3
Moderately important	83	39.3
Not very important	62	29.4
Total	211*	100.0

*Number of women who responded to this question.

important to either quality or permanence; their opinions are distributed along the entire continuum. A few more women think sex is importantly related to quality; a few less think it importantly related to permanence. But close to a third of the women fall in each of the three categories for both questions.

I also wondered how satisfied long-term lesbian couples are with their sexual relationship. Table 4.5 shows the responses the women gave to this question. Again the nine-point scale has been reduced to three categories.

Nearly 60 percent of lesbians in long-term couples

TABLE 4.5 SATISFACTION WITH SEXUAL RELATIONSHIP

Degree of importance	Number of women	Percent of women
Very satisfied	123	58.9
Moderately satisfied	51	24.4
Not very satisfied	35	16.7
Total	209*	100.0

*Number of women who responded to this question.

155

are very satisfied with the sexual relationship they have with their partners. In fact 13.9 percent are extremely satisfied (Response = 1). Remember, however, that being very satisfied does not necessarily mean the couple is being very sexual. They may both be satisfied with the nonsexual nature of their relationship.

Comparing the women's satisfaction with sex with how often they and their partner were sexual shows a weak positive correlation (r = .366), i.e., the more sexual, the more satisfied, and vice versa. Women in couples who are at least as sexual as the norm for long-term relationships in this study, two to three times per month, are rarely dissatisfied with their sexual relationship. By contrast, the twelve women who are the most dissatisfied (Responses = 8 or 9 on the scale) — all have sex once a month or less. There are, however, nine women who have not had sex in the past year who are extremely satisfied with their sexual relationship (Response = 1).

The relationship between your sense of satisfaction and the frequency of sex between you and your partner is obviously a matter of personal and couple preference. The challenge is to find the amount (and quality) of sex that best satisfies both of you.

I compared the individuals in each couple to see whether they agreed about their degree of satisfaction. Mostly they do; 78.7 percent of the couples are in close or fairly close agreement. But 21.3 percent of the couples are in fairly great or great disagreement about how satisfied they are.

One such couple, Cynthia and Gail, have been together ten years and are both in their middle 40s. Cynthia considers them lovers, reports that the frequency of sexual contact has decreased since the beginning of their relationship, but the quality has remained the same. They have not had sex in the past two years. She is very satisfied, a response = 2 on the scale.

Her partner Gail no longer considers them lovers, says both the frequency and the quality have decreased since the beginning, and underscores that it has been two years since they made love. She is very dissatisfied, a response of 9 on the scale. When I ask her about how important their sexual life is to the quality or permanence of their relationship, she says, "I guess it's not important; we don't have one!"

I think it is rare that sex alone constitutes a problem in a couple relationship. It is clear from reading all the questionnaire entries for this couple that they are troubled in more than just their sex life. For instance, I ask each woman "What would you say is the single biggest source of problems for you and your partner in your relationship?"

> *Cynthia:* I cry too much when we have differences. I don't talk enough.
>
> *Gail:* Communication. My partner keeps things to herself, doesn't discuss when she's upset with me and why. I stopped discussing things personal or emotional because she cries and nothing gets settled. Then I feel like a crumb. Now whatever it is goes unsaid.

Both Cynthia and Gail mention being friends as well as lovers as one of the three most significant factors that explain why they have stayed together. Cynthia puts it third; Gail first.

When they talk about what forms the heart of a successful relationship, Cynthia says, among other things, "Communication, openness at all levels from trivial to major." Gail says "Trust. Caring for each other."

You can see that at this point in their long relationship, this couple has serious disagreements about the communication between them, how open it is, who is talking, who is not, etc. Sexuality may be just one more form of communication that has broken down.

Everyone in the study agrees that the early period of intense sexuality when we are first forming our lesbian couple relationships moderates after a time. "The honeymoon ends, but the relationship enters a new phase, requiring work and giving, exploration of all the other reasons you chose this partner." (10-year couple) If the honeymoon is gone, what *is* left of sexuality, in a quantitative sense? I asked "How often during the last year have you and your partner had sexual relations?" Table 4.6 reports the frequency of sexual contact.

After at least ten years of living together, these lesbian couples make love, most typically, two to three times per month. A naturopath friend of mine says, "Of course: two women, two ovulations per month with attendant hormone changes, two sexual encounters." (Are we truly just life-sized expressions of our body chemistry?) There is a great deal of variability, however, in the amount of sex these long-term couples enjoy. Twenty-five women are making love one to two times per week while fifteen

TABLE 4.6 FREQUENCY OF SEXUAL CONTACT IN PAST YEAR

How often . . .?	Number of women	Percent of women
Daily, almost every day	0	0.0
3, 4 times per week	0	0.0
1, 2 times per week	25	12.6
2, 3 times per month	57	28.8
Once per month	33	16.7
Once every few months	32	16.2
A few times during the year	15	7.6
No sexual relations during the year	36	18.2
Total	198*	100.0

*Number of women who responded to this question.

are making love just a few times a year. Eighteen percent of the women have not made love in the last year, which, from my experience interviewing these women, means they have probably stopped making love altogether.

Phil Blumstein and Pepper Schwartz, the sociologists who studied American couples, have some data we can use to compare with mine. They calculated which of their couples who had been together ten years or more had sex once a month or less. They found that 15 percent of married couples had sex this infrequently, 33 percent of gay men, and 47 percent of lesbians. Looking at their data as a whole they conclude, "Lesbians have sex less frequently by far than any other type of couple, and they do not have a compensating rate of sex outside the relationship." (*American Couples,* page 195)

Blumstein and Schwartz speculate that the low level of genital sexuality in lesbians may be due — in part — to the socialization of women. Women are taught to be the receivers of sexual advances, men are taught to be the initiators. If no male is present, the problem of who is to initiate sexual contact arises. Both being women, each waits for her partner to do so.

A 12-year couple, who make love two to three times per month, foresee such possible problems: "There is no role to rely on . . . it must carry itself. We must both desire sex or we don't have any, and I could see women get 'lazy' about making it happen."

There is another way lesbian sexuality may suffer from our hesitancy to be initiators. One of the things I found repeatedly in the couples I interviewed who no longer make love is that some kind of event interrupted their sexual life. I particularly think of bouts of ill health as being the precipitating cause, although many kinds of trauma intervened, hurtful affairs being another principal one. Once the crisis had passed, these couples did not resume being sexual. Both partners were willing to let that part of their lives together go; neither partner felt compelled to re-initiate sexual contact.

Schwartz and Blumstein also report that "lesbian couples prize nongenital physical contact — cuddling, touching, hugging — probably more than other couples do. But more important, they are much more likely to consider these activities as ends in themselves, rather than as foreplay leading to genital sex." (*American Couples*, page 197) As we know, this is true of the women in our long-term couples. As is another finding of the sociologists: "Lesbians do not feel less satisfied with their relationships when sex occurs infrequently." (*American Couples,* page 201) Based on my study, I should add: on the whole. Some lesbians are very dissatisfied with infrequent sex.

Couples for Whom Sex Is Important

Barbara and Margie, an eleven-year couple, are 50 and 41 years old. They have raised Margie's two children from a previous marriage for ten of these eleven years together.

Barbara says sex is the second most significant thing that explains why they have stayed together. Love is the first, commitment the third. Margie describes what she thinks forms the heart of a successful relationship: "Sharing mutual values: same priorities for work, children, time. Loving each other and having a physical attraction for each other. Similar outlook on life."

They both talk about sex when responding to the questions about the joys and pleasures of their relationship:

> *Barbara:* Sex, doing things together, being with other lesbian couples, being with the kids.
> *Margie:* The fun we have together. Sex. Friendship.

This couple makes love once or twice a week, a good deal higher than the lesbian average. They are both satisfied and say their sex life is important to the quality and the permanence of their relationship. Frequency has declined, quality has increased.

161

A twelve-year couple, Laurel and Karen, are in their early forties. They have had a lot of serious problems in their relationship: an early affair, a two-month breakup, alcoholism. None has damaged their sexual relationship. They make love two to three times a month, are very satisfied, and feel sex is important to quality and permanence. They are monogamous. Asked about joys and pleasures, they say:

> *Laurel:* We both are still "head over heels" in love with each other! We both have a good sense of humor. We have mutual interests and appreciate the same things. We have fun with each other, and she's my best friend.
>
> *Karen:* We appreciate each other's intelligence, beauty, and talents . . . Also, I feel our sexual relationship is very good. We feel comfortable in that area and have never experienced such pleasure with anyone else.

Carla is 53, Jean 55. Their's is a fourteen-year relationship, one in which sex is very important. They are sexual once or twice a week.

> *Susan:* Do you think sex is particularly important to you? Do you make special efforts in that direction?
>
> *Carla:* It seems to come natural, doesn't it? Perhaps because we're both healthy, and active people.
>
> *Susan:* Have either of you gone through menopause yet?

Jean: I have.

Susan: Has that affected your being sexual at all?

Jean: I don't think there's any difference.

Carla: I think that together we are still learning about things that are nice to do sexually.

Jean: Well, I think you're a sexy person.

Carla: I have all those feelings; I act them out. I act on what I feel about everything, sometimes to my detriment. I think if you're alive and well and healthy, then your sex life should be alive and well and healthy too. If it isn't, I should think you would want to do something, you know, talking with each other about it. We do, from time to time.

Jean: We've done a lot of talking about it.

Carla: If you were having a problem and you kept it to yourself, then I suppose you might quit having sex. But we usually talk about things. Everything.

This next couple also tell us about the importance of talking in maintaining an intimate sexual relationship. When I interviewed them, Rena, 40, and Mattie, 33, had just gone through two of the hardest years in their twelve-year relationship. Among a myriad of catastrophes, Rena had been nearly crippled with back problems and then undergone major surgery.

Susan: When you say you coped very well, what do you mean specifically?

163

Rena: Well, one thing is that when we get to fighting, we need to be touching each other. If we can't have sex, we need to be touching each other. As far as sex was concerned, it was sort of a lost memory. She was sick, my back was out, neither of us felt like it.

Susan: How long did you go without being sexual?

Mattie: We could never go for very long, but, let's see. . . .

Rena: It must have been almost three months.

Mattie: That doesn't mean that we didn't touch. We figured out, if we can't be sexual, we need to touch, to hold each other and snuggle.

Susan: Did it feel like an effort, to get back to being sexual?

Mattie: We had a plan. It sounds so clinical.

Susan: No. It's important.

Mattie: We talked about the fact that it had been a long time and what our needs were and what Rena felt capable of . . .

Rena: How we could do it!

Mattie: How we could do it.

Rena: We talked about it throughout too, cause you'd say "I'll be glad when your back gets better!"

Mattie: We made appointments to get together, and kind of courted a little bit too. Cause once you're layin' in bed, and you think, "This is it." Well, it ain't it. You may be too scared by this time.

Rena: Awkward.

Mattie: It was very awkward. And too scary, if you haven't led up to it. Cause we'd been through periods of no sex like this before, so we know that we need to . . .

Rena: Talk.

Mattie: Talk, and then court each other, like dates and flowers.

Rena: Interrupt our daily routine.

Mattie: So we had to have dates and stuff. Kind of lead up to it. Cause just to say, "Okay, everything's over, let's do it!" No, no. We couldn't do that. We had to reestablish ourselves as lovers.

Rena and Mattie are saying that they kept touching and kept talking. They were physical with each other even if they weren't genital. They talked about being sexual, even when they weren't able to be and didn't feel like it. They explicitly talked about and looked forward to a time when they would be sexual again. Then, when they both felt better, they talked about how they would reintroduce sexuality into their lives. It didn't just happen. They needed to take special steps to get past the awkwardness — the fear — that had built up over the months they weren't sexual.

Being sexual is a very intimate experience. Opening up to this kind of vulnerability again after being closed for a while may not be something we can expect ourselves to do without effort and attention. Making the effort, though, is crucial, if you want to become lovers again. Making the effort together, by talking and courting, is a giant step in being intimate, the kind of intimacy that can climax in being sexual again.

Sexual Frequency Related to Age and Longevity

It is common to observe that sexual energy diminishes with age. Likewise we all experience sexual frequency declining with the longevity of a relationship. But does this mean that the older you are, the less likely you are to be sexual? And that the older your relationship is, the less likely you are to be sexual together?

In general, the answer is yes to both these questions. This study found a positive correlation (r = .413) between the age of the women and the frequency of sex in their relationships: the older, the less frequent. A positive correlation (r = .349) also shows up between the length of the relationship and the frequency of sex: the older the relationship, the less frequent the sex. Note, however, that both these correlations are relatively weak; there is a relationship, but not a strong relationship.

Because age of the women and longevity of the couple are related to each other (in general, older women have been in their couples longer), I also compared all three variables simultaneously: age, longevity, and sexual frequency. I wanted to see (1) what effect the age of the partners had on sexual frequency regardless of how long a couple has been together, and (2) what effect longevity has on sexual frequency regardless of how old the partners are.

Age is the more significant factor. The correlation between age and sexual frequency (with longevity held constant) is .253; the correlation between longevity and sexual frequency (with age held constant) is only .109. Thus, the impact of age on how often long-term lesbian couples make love is stronger than the impact of how long the couple has been together — in general. Again, however, what is equally important is how weak both relationships are.

What the data show is that, although as lesbians age they are less likely to have sex, there are lesbians of every age who have frequent sex, and lesbians of every age who have little sex. Age is not a determining factor. You (and your partner) are the determining factor.

The picture is the same for the relationship between the longevity of a couple and the frequency of sexual contact. The amount of sex you and your partner enjoy is influenced by how long you have been together, but it need not be determined by this. If you both want to be sexual, neither advancing age nor accumulating longevity need prevent you. If neither of you wants to be sexual, neither youth nor newness of the relationship will compel you.

Couples for Whom Sex Is Not Important

Not everyone in long-term lesbian couples cares about being sexual, in the sense of genitally, orgasmically sexual. In fact, it was not uncommon for women who are no longer being sexual to tell me they find nonsexuality a superior state: "Our love has

167

grown so that we don't need physical expression like that."

This particular remark was made by Pamela, a 63-year-old woman whose relationship has lasted seventeen years, the last six or so without sexual contact. She and her 66-year-old partner, Monica, discussed the process of diminishing sexual interest. They were both nurses before they retired and thus focus on the physiological concomitants.

Pamela: We knew you were coming to interview, and that we'd both put down on the questionnaires that we don't have sex anymore, so just the other day I asked Monica, "Do you miss sex?" She looked right at me and said, "No, I don't." I felt a little like, "Why not?" She said, "Do you?" And actually I don't. (Laughter) But, you know . . .

Susan: Do you think you should miss it?

Pamela: I think I should. It kinda bothered me. So we talked about it awhile, and Monica said, "Remember, we went off estrogen. Don't you think maybe our hormone levels are down?" And then we both have atrophic vaginitis, which means the vaginal tract is drawing and getting fragile, nonelastic.

Susan: Is that because you're not lubricating as much any more?

Pamela: All those things gradually happen at the same time. And yes, one of the functions of estrogen is it keeps everything lubricated. And it helps your sexual energy too, your libido.

Susan: Were you real sexual at first, when your relationship first began?

Monica: Yes.

Pamela: For several years, three? four? five?

Monica: At least.

Pamela: And then it got to be less frequent and less frequent and eventually just dropped off. And then one New Year's, maybe about six years ago — we hadn't had sex for about year — we had sex again. And it did seem, maybe not as Cloud Nineish, but the feeling was there, just not as much so.

Susan: Did you talk about that, about sex becoming less and less, as it was happening? Were you aware of it?

Monica: Oh, yeah.

Pamela and Monica remembered this New Year's because around the same time they had remodeled the bedrooms in their house. One took the downstairs, and one the upstairs bedroom.

Susan: Did the room separation reflect the fact that sexuality had fallen off?

Pamela: Yeah, I'd buy that. I think that's probably part of it. But you know, the aging process somehow . . . you get so your bones don't lay as well even if you've got a queen-size bed.

Monica: You just don't rest.

169

Later I asked if they were physically affectionate.

Pamela: Not a great deal now.
Monica: Not a great deal. From time to time.
Like when we're around other couples.

I am struck by several things in this story. One is how this couple experienced lessened sexuality as a simultaneous lessening of their physical affection in general. This is unusual among the non-sexual couples I interviewed; many are still physically affectionate and find that contact important. I also notice that Pamela and Monica are more physically affectionate around other lesbian couples. It's almost as if they are reminded of their lesbianism and encouraged to express it by their friends. Otherwise, they easily slip into a purely companion-style relationship.

The other major thing of interest to me here is the impact physiology can have on different lesbians. Monica and Pamela experienced a distinct, though gradual, decline in sexual energy with the aftermath of menopause. Several other women reported the same thing. Ginny had a hysterectomy at age 44 and, as she puts it, "They took my horny away." As it turns out, though, the hysterectomy was only one among many traumatic events — a move, the death of her partner Virginia's father, and Ginny's mother, all in about six months. Ginny: "And I never recovered." Both now say they're okay with less sex. They make love every other month or so, and they agree, "Thank God we both feel the same way, or we'd be in a world of hurt."

Sometimes the desire not to be sexual originates

with one partner only, and this creates a painful situation which, of course, must be resolved if the couple is to continue. Esther, age 64, and Suzanne, age 51, have been together nineteen years. It was about ten years ago that Esther became disillusioned with being sexual. This attitude coincided with her menopause, so again physiology may have had an impact. But this couple — or at least one partner of this couple — experienced the change as spiritual, not physical.

> *Esther:* I think we had a really nice, passionate affair at the start. And I think it just got nicer and better with time. And she's certainly the best, most considerate lover I have ever had. So we had a nice sex life. And then . . .
>
> *Suzanne:* And then it happened.
>
> *Esther:* And then I got to feeling that this having sex is all very pleasant, but it takes a lot of energy. And I wanted to direct this energy some other way because I found sex ultimately disappointing in the end. So we don't have any sex now; we have quite a lot of affection. I don't know whether I'm mainly to blame for that, but I think so.
>
> *Susan:* Did you discuss it at the time?
>
> *Esther:* I know we talked about it some, and I think your feelings were hurt, Suzanne. But the thing is, I wanted things to mean something. You have sex, and you have sex, and you have sex, and it's all very pleasant, but it seemed empty to me, meaningless; there didn't seem to be any point to it.

Susan: Like it wasn't going anywhere?

Esther: Yeah. I mean, where is it gonna go? Maybe there is somewhere for it to go, but I couldn't find it.

Suzanne: No, it is what it is. It doesn't have anyplace to go.

A bit later in the interview,

Susan: Suzanne, how did you feel about all this?

Suzanne: I was not able to hear it as anything but rejection. I didn't understand it, I didn't like it.

(She talks to Esther) You used to talk about it in terms of wanting to have a deeper relationship, and that I had some barrier to that, and so the sexuality had no point. I always heard that your sadness had to do with me; it was my fault, somehow or other.

I had to go through feeling really lonely, I felt sorry for myself. And I pretty much kept my struggles to myself for maybe a couple of years. But I was busy, I was doing other things. . . . I have never considered myself a very sexual being, it never was the driving force of my life.

I still once in a while think how nice it was, you know, but I no longer wish I had it back or anything like that, because whether we would have sexual relating or not has absolutely nothing to do with my feelings about Esther.

172

Still later,

> *Suzanne:* I think that the main thing is that sex should be put into some kind of perspective in a person's life. So much more of your life has value. You should concern yourself with whether you can talk nice to the person you're living with, not whether you're gonna have sex that night.
>
> *Esther:* Sex tends to be a lot less important to lesbians than it is to either heterosexuals or gay men. And I think that's wonderful because I think that's a very freeing thing.

This story highlights the painful adaptations women who want to remain in long-term couples may have to make. Suzanne adjusted to Esther's not wanting to be sexual anymore, but the adjustment was not easy. And we are hearing about it ten years after the event, when the hurt has had a chance to dissipate.

Menopause is also relevant to this story, though it is impossible to sort out which comes first, the physiology or the psychology and spirituality. There is no question that the biology of sex has something to do with the frequency and quality of sex among lesbians, but just how that biological response expresses itself varies tremendously. Remember that Jean, introduced earlier in this chapter as one of the women in a couple for whom sex is important (Carla and Jean), experienced menopause without any change in her sexual response. Dotty and Martha, the two church women who took ten years to get together, fell in love just as they were becoming menopausal.

Their first years together were just as sexual as anyone younger might experience.

I think we can conclude that, though aging and its attendant biological changes are distinctly a factor, especially for some women, the precise impact of these changes depends on the woman herself, her partner, and how important sex has been to the relationship independent of biology.

Other factors prove inhibitory of sexual expression for lesbians. For a few, the impact of religious proscription is critical. (For a very few, I would guess. Many who feel as strongly as Mary Frances would never become lesbians at all.)

Mary Frances and Cecille are in their late 70s, and have been together forty-one years. They were sexual, or at least intensely sensual, once, at the very beginning of their relationship, when they were falling in love. But Mary Frances is a devout Catholic, and her religious convictions would not allow her to continue their relationship as a sexual relationship. She told me about the sweetness of their falling in love,

> *Mary Frances:* We were at camp, sitting together on these stone steps by a stream, a beautiful place. Getting closer and closer to knowing each other. And I knew right then, I knew that we belonged together. Then later, it was a rainy night, and we slept together in the same bunk, and you know, we just felt intimate enough to hug and kiss each other, and that was all. That's it.

Susan: Were you ever any more sexual than that in your relationship?

Mary Frances: One time. But I didn't feel entitled. I was told by the church I was not entitled, and I would never have been happy if we had continued.

Forty-one years later she concludes,

Mary Frances: I have a sense of security in the knowledge that we were meant to be together. Hugs and kisses are treats. Everyday living is shared with confidence. Our life is not punctuated with regrets.

Her partner, Cecille, tells her side:

Cecille: Because of my partner's religious beliefs, she did not want to base our relationship on sex. Although this was extremely difficult for me at first, I am glad now that this was so.

This couple attributes their longevity, at least in part, to the fact that they were (almost) never sexual:

Cecille: We had to depend on other things to bring us closer together. We didn't just have an awareness of doing without. We paid attention to all the other things that go to make up a close relationship; we devoted our lives to other things.

We have been there for each other, in many, many different ways. Always.

A variety of crises can interrupt a couple's sexual life: ill health; the deaths of people significant to one or both partners; other losses, like a job or a move; affairs and separations. If sex is important for a couple, they can work their way back to being sexual again. But some couples let these interruptions become permanent. What may be happening is that the crisis becomes a convenient way to stop an activity that already has lost its excitement and pull on the couple.

Lori, 41, and Eleanor, 52, illustrate this pattern. They are a nineteen-year couple who have never gotten back to being sexual after Eleanor's successful recovery from heart surgery four or five years ago. But they really date their diminishing interest in being sexual to before that time.

> *Lori:* I think we're physically very close; sexually it's died off.
> *Eleanor:* From sex being every night to none. We haven't had physical sex in, oh, three, four years. We've talked about it . . .
> *Lori:* Oh, yeah, we talk about it. But it doesn't seem important to either one of us.
> *Eleanor:* The sleeping together, the sleeping spoon fashion, the being able to touch, the physical closeness is real important. But the actual sex act seems absolutely irrelevant.

I talked with this couple about the importance of sex at the beginning of relationships. They disagree about its importance.

> *Susan:* It's interesting that sex falls off so

much when it's usually so important at first. If you hadn't been sexual at first, do you think it would have made a big difference in your relationship?

Lori: Nah, I don't think it would've made any difference. But I don't know that. My sense is, though, that it wouldn't have.

Eleanor: I can't imagine a relationship starting without sex. I really can't. That's what makes it unique and different from other relationships. It changes that feeling of love. I certainly have love for many of my friends, and a real close love and longing to hug them and be near them, but the sexual feeling isn't there . . . For me there would have to be that sexual component to kind of cement the relationship at the beginning.

Lori and Eleanor typify a couple for whom sex was critical at the beginning of the relationship as a bonding experience. Now, nineteen years later, being sexual has lost its fascination. Although sex is no longer important for them, monogamy is. Eleanor: "We'd have one hell of a restructuring if either of us got sexually involved with another person! The practice of being sexual may not remain important in a relationship, but the exclusivity still is."

How Couples Deal with Monogamy/Non-monogamy

Any couple that stays together a long time has probably had to deal with the issue of sexual

177

exclusiveness or openness in the relationship, i.e., the issue of monogamy/non-monogamy. I asked each women about this issue in a question with a series of fairly detailed alternative responses:

Question: Which *one* of the following statements best describes you and your partner's current understanding concerning sex outside of your relationship?

Possible responses:

1. We have discussed it and decided that under *some* circumstances it is all right.
2. We have discussed it and decided that under *no* circumstances is it all right.
3. We have discussed it and do not agree. (I then asked each woman to explain how she feels.)
4. We have *not* discussed it but I feel we would agree that under *some* circumstances it is all right.
5. We have *not* discussed it but I feel we would agree that under *no* circumstances is it all right.
6. We have *not* discussed it but I feel that we would not agree. (Please explain)

Thus, the woman had the choices of: (1) whether she and her partner had discussed the issue; (2) whether they agreed on the issue; and (3) if they agreed, whether that agreement allowed sex outside the relationship.

I then combined the responses of the partners to

TABLE 4.7 COUPLE AGREEMENTS ABOUT MONOGAMY/NON-MONOGAMY

The partners in this couple have . . .	Number of couples	Percent of couples
Discussed and agree to *some* circumstances	11	10.4
Discussed and agree to *no* circumstances	59	55.7
Discussed and disagree	15	14.2
Not discussed, but agree they would agree to *some* circumstances	0	0.0
Not discussed, but agree they would agree to *no* circumstances	7	6.6
Not discussed, and disagree	2	1.9
Do not agree either to discussing it or to how they feel	5	4.7
Do not agree about discussing it, but do agree on how they feel	3	2.8
Other	4	3.8
Total	106*	100.0

*Number of couples who responded to this question.

calculate how each couple felt about the issue. Table 4.7 gives these couple responses.

It may not be easy to come to a resolution of this issue. You can see that seven of the nine responses involve couples either not discussing the issue, not agreeing, neither discussing nor agreeing, or other, which means the response was unclassifiably unique.

One of my favorite instances of non-agreement had to do with the questionnaires from a couple, both

179

of whom were therapists. As therapists are wont to do, they emphasized the importance of good communication throughout their responses. And, as you by now suspect, when I came to the monogamy/non-monogamy question, one therapist responded "under some circumstances," the other, "under no circumstances, unless renegotiated."

Amused by the fallibility of all of us, I reported this disagreement, unsuspected by the parties involved, to my partner Connie, a therapist herself. The next morning we had this exchange:

> *Connie:* Susan, we do have an agreement about monogamy, don't we?
> *Susan:* Yes, dear, we do.
> *Connie:* And that agreement is, is it not, that under no circumstances is it okay to be sexual outside our relationship?
> *Susan:* Yes, darling, that's our agreement.
> *Connie:* Good . . . just checking.

A sizeable majority (55.7 percent) of the couples in this study have discussed the issue of sex outside their relationship and have agreed that under no circumstances is this all right. Another 6.6 percent have not discussed the issue, but agree that they have an implicit agreement that under no circumstances is it all right.

These monogamous agreements may be reached in a variety of ways. Many women share an intense commitment to this principle:

> "I do not believe that sex is okay outside the relationship, and I love my partner enough

180

that I don't ever want her to hurt because of me." (Sarah, age 45, a 19-year couple)

Some women come to a commitment gradually, but when they do, it is firm, and monogamy is probably its base. Bonnie, age 36, makes an articulate statement of the rationale for monogamy from her vantage point of ten years in her relationship:

"It took me a long time (four years) to make a lifelong commitment. When I did, I really meant it. I had made a temporary commitment to Martha and monogamy during the first four years.

"Making a commitment actually gives me more freedom because it sets my boundaries about other relationships. There is no confusion so I'm free to develop friendships or work relationships.

"I am more secure because I know Martha is committed to me, and her friendships and work relationships are just that. I encourage her to develop them.

"It wasn't until I felt secure in my and Martha's commitment to each other that I could totally let my defenses down and show her that I really needed her to love me with all my fears and concerns. I distinctly remember a shift from holding and taking care of Martha to letting her hold me and take care of me.

"I don't believe this could happen in a non-monogamous relationship because the security is not there."

Lesbian couples also may arrive at their agreement about monogamy from having experimented with the alternative. I asked the women in these couples if they had ever considered breaking up, and if so, the reasons for considering it, and why they didn't break up in the end. Eighty-two percent of the women say they have considered a break-up at some time in the course of their relationship. Of this 82 percent, 27.8 percent considered breaking up principally because she or her partner had an affair, fell in love with someone else, etc.

"We almost broke up at year seven after my lover had an affair with my best friend. We didn't break up because we were committed to each other and sought help from two therapists." (14-year couple)

"Other rough times were when we experimented with non-monogamy. It created conflicts and strained our relationship. We finally decided the temporary thrills weren't worth the hassles, although we both always felt our relationship was the primary and lasting one." (15-year couple)

A twenty-year couple said it succinctly: "Momentary affairs made for burdensome complexities," and, her partner: "Non-monogamy made for monstrous scenarios. Back to monogamy." Here is another version of the same story, told in more detail. This couple had been together fourteen years, and got together when they were both 16 years old, each other's first significant relationship. Now they are 30, with a lot of experimentation behind them.

"The time that I think was the most traumatic was when I had an affair with another woman at the end of our first year together. I never viewed it as a 'replacement' relationship. Actually, I guess it was more of an experiment in open marriage. For about four months I lived with my partner, but spent a couple of nights a week with the other woman.

"We all agreed to the rules set up ahead of time before I became involved with her, but it was *still* hell for everybody. Of course, she wanted more time with me and not to feel used. My partner tried to be understanding but was deeply hurt. I was confused, torn, and wasn't having *any fun!* Soon I just wanted out of the mess.

(She describes several more affairs. . . .)

"Throughout all of these indiscretions we talked constantly about our feelings and motivations. There are still scars — and overall, it wasn't worth it. That's how I feel now about affairs — they never are uncomplicated or unpainful. They just aren't worth all the trouble they cause."

Though what a couple thinks about monogamy/non-monogamy is important, the partners, even in long-term couples, do not always agree. In fact, 20.8 percent of the couples in this study did not agree about monogamy, some having talked about it and

183

disagreeing (14.2 percent), some not having talked about it and disagreeing (1.9 percent), and some not agreeing either to having talked about it or to how they feel about it (4.7 percent). Here are some descriptions of these disagreements:

"I think that casual sexual interaction (at a conference for example) is OK. She does not agree. She does not want any extra-curricular sex, for her or for me." (11-year couple)

"She feels in no circumstances would (sex outside the relationship) be appropriate. I feel with some structure it could be okay (although I've never tested it so I'm not certain!).

"I feel a nagging need to experience other women, as I was only 21 when we got together and had never really dated or been sexual with anyone else. This is a constant source of tension in our relationship." (14-year couple)

"I think an infatuation with someone else can best be solved with the freedom to indulge in sex if that's indicated. Jean says, 'pack your bags if you do.' So I don't. But I'd like to, now and again." (14-year couple)

I was curious as to whether or not couples with more longevity are more likely to agree about monogamy. This seems not to be the case. Just as many couples (proportionately) who have been together fifteen years or more are in disagreement about this issue as are couples who've been together ten to fourteen years. Even a few couples who've been together a very long time do not agree.

What of the couples who are non-monogamous, who agree that sex outside their relationship is all right. Seven of these eleven couples have agreements that I call "non-monogamy of the mind." This means they agree in principle that outside sexual contact is okay, but they've never acted on it.

Sometimes these situations can be very painful, because they represent an uneasy and never-challenged status quo. Kim and Mel come to mind. These women have been together eighteen years, and throughout that time have been unable to either lay to rest or act upon their differing feelings about sexuality in general and non-monogamy in particular. Mel is Kim's first and only woman lover. Mel has had one previous female lover. Each has been involved significantly with a man. Mel is 39, Kim, 37 years old.

> *Susan:* You said in your questionnaires that you have an agreement that you could be non-monogamous. Tell me about that.
>
> *Mel:* After we did the questionnaires, we talked about affairs. Neither one of us has had them.
>
> *Kim:* I would like one.
>
> *Mel:* Kim would like one. We have always decided that in the event that were to happen, we would want the other one to tell that it had happened and we would deal with it then.
>
> *Kim:* I've had a couple of opportunities. I

think the primary reason I haven't done it is that I wasn't absolutely positive that it wouldn't jeopardize my relationship with Mel. And much as I wanted to act on it, I thought I was paying a pretty big price if we as a couple couldn't work it out, even though I'm pretty convinced we could. But I'll probably go to my grave, if I never have some kind of affair or fling, regretting it.

Susan: And how would you feel, Mel, if Kim had an affair?

Mel: I don't know. I think I would have to wait and see. A lot would depend on who it was.

Kim: If I was convinced that it would have no long-term effects whatsoever on my relationship with Mel, I'd be doing it. We can talk all we want, but we've never really tested that particular water.

Also, I think if I'm sleeping with somebody, I'm probably going to fall in love with that person. And I don't want that to happen either. And I just wouldn't want to hurt Mel. I think no matter what, it would be very hurtful.

Mel: Oh, I didn't say it wouldn't hurt.

And so they go, around and around, with the issue never really resolving itself, Kim feeling constrained and regretful, Mel maintaining her stoicism.

Non-monogamy of the mind is important to some long-term lesbian couples. I believe it gives one or both partners a feeling of relative freedom, the idea that *if* they wanted to be involved with someone else

— under the perfect circumstances, of course — they could be. They need not feel "imprisoned" by their commitment to their partner.

What of the couples who are actively non-monogamous? There are four such couples among the 108 couples in the group.

One is a couple of ten years where one woman has maintained a sexual relationship with the father of her two children for nine and a half years. Though their questionnaires indicate several serious problems in this relationship, none are directly attributable to the long-term triangle they have maintained.

Margery, age 71, and Kathryn, age 69, are another non-monogamous couple. They have been celibate with each other for twenty of their twenty-four years together. During this time they have both experienced significant sexual relationships with other women, women who are considered part of their extended family.

> Margery: The first time it was a secret, and it was a disaster. Kath's no good at keeping secrets, anyhow. And I think that's what hurt me more than . . . well, we got that settled; everybody cried a lot.
> Kathryn: Confidentiality is the root of all evil, I always say.
> Margery: So, after that, we each always knew what the other was doing. (She thinks about one of her outside partners.) I wish I could put Kath and Alice in a blender, turn the blender on and I'd have the perfect person! Because all the things that Kath loves to do are exactly the opposite of

187

Alice, and vice versa . . . About twice a year Alice and I'd have a real going-away, we'd do interesting things, and so on.

And Kath has kept a long-term relationship with a friend up north for years. It's no longer sexual, but she's a part of our family. She and her kids. We just never had those boundaries.

Susan: It's very interesting that you can sustain those long outside relationships. A lot of people think . . .

Margery: Think they can.

Kathryn talks about her longest outside relationship.

Kathryn: I think for me it was a fortunate accident that the other person I loved, again not in a very sexual sense, I also got to work with for years. I spent most of my work time with her at the same time I was living with Margery. She was sort of the other half of my life. (To Margery) I think it was not a relationship that you even resented, you were good friends with her.

Margery: I was and still am very fond of her. I think the only jealousy I felt was in relation to Sue, which was that first time, when it was a secret. And then, as I said, we all cried a lot . . . you didn't cry much; I cried a lot. And then it was like, Well, this is the way it's going to be. You can't own anybody, you cannot put your whole life into one other person . . . Sometimes I feel sad about it.

Susan: Sad about what?

Margery: About not having a sexual relationship with someone, but . . .

Susan: You mean with Kathryn in particular, or . . .

Margery: Yes, I think with Kathryn. Sometimes I feel well, maybe it's cheating (that they're not sexual with each other), but we love each other in ways that are very supportive and comforting. We sleep together all the time.

Susan: I was going to ask you about nongenital kinds of touching.

Margery: Our touching is all nongenital, and I figure Kath would tell me if it was intolerable, and it doesn't seem to be. I'm just saying what I feel about this; we don't talk about it to each other. We did earlier . . .

Kathryn: Not much to talk about.

In a third non-monogamous couple, together fourteen years, one partner has been having an affair for three years. The other partner, while tolerating the situation, is not happy with it.

Nan: My partner feels she sometimes needs sex elsewhere. I don't, and don't like the fact that she does, but . . . the alternative is worse.

Nan is philosophical. In response to the question about what is their single biggest source of problems, she says, "The outside woman, but that will pass away."

Her partner, Judith, explains, "Nan would like me to stop seeing Margot. I can't do that now." This couple makes love once a month (Nan) or once every few months (Judith), depending on who is estimating, and both are relatively dissatisfied with their sexual relationship.

Though clearly a non-monogamous relationship that both partners know about and tolerate, this couple does not agree that the arrangement is a good idea. In fact, with apologies for presumptuousness to the previous two couples, I get the sense that those couples' non-monogamous arrangements were — like Nan and Judith's — originally adaptations on the part of one partner to the needs of the other. They were not happy arrangements arrived at because both women felt an equal desire for other sexual partners.

The fourth non-monogamous relationship comes perhaps the closest to feeling of true comfort on the part of both partners. Shirley and Joanna have been a non-monogamous couple for the twelve years of their relationship. They have a 15-year-old daughter from Shirley's prior marriage. They offer this advice:

Shirley: Don't merge. Don't try to conform to the nuclear family model; it was set up by a few men.
Joanna: Believe in yourself and your feelings even when the odds are against you.

This couple credits the presence of Shirley's daughter with keeping them together at one crucial point in their relationship. (The break-up point had nothing to do with their non-monogamy.)

> *Shirley:* One time we almost broke up was when my lover first started dealing with childhood incest memories. I was dealing with learning not to be a caretaker. We would have at least stopped living together for a while, but it was clear to both of us that that would be bad for our child. As for what kept us together, all I can say is perseverance.
>
> *Joanna:* When I was deeply depressed and asexual, she was in love with someone else, and our daughter was a bitch. We stayed together because of our daughter's needs, not feeling finished, still loving each other, and not wanting to end the relationship.

Two of the other non-monogamous couples have children as well. The first couple's non-monogamy centers around the father of the couple's two children. The third couple, Judith and Nan, have a son.

> *Judith:* When I became involved with Margot three years ago, I thought about leaving Nan. I didn't because of our son (who made it very clear that he didn't want our family broken up) and because, despite my other involvement, I really love her.

Thus, three of the four non-monogamous couples have children they are raising. I am reluctant, however, to conclude firmly that it is the presence of children that solidifies these non-monogamous couples. In Chapter 6, Children, Family and Friends, the women who know tell us children can be as divisive an influence as they can be cohesive.

Writing this chapter is painful. I keep feeling all the anguish underneath the brave words. I remember how difficult it was for these women to talk with each other in front of me about a subject that may have left scars. It was the rare interview where sex in the couples's life was such a source of pure joy that talking about it was fun. Pure joy at first, yes, when the couple got together. But by now, almost every couple has been through something about sexuality that has proven very hard, if only the realization that — much as we wish it weren't so — passion cools.

What saves us is that, though passion cools, affection — deep affection — remains. These women love to love.

And we're saved by something else as well: our sensuality. Despite everything, these lesbians love to look, to listen, to smell, to touch.

"I enjoy my partner's company. I feel secure in her presence. It pleases me to watch her interact with others. I love to hear the stories she tells about her day and the people she encounters. I am excited to accomplish simple tasks or major projects side-by-side with her. I like sharing the task of preparing lists of things for us to do and making plans for our future.

"I enjoy riding in the car in silence with my hand on her thigh. I thrill to watch her undress. I love to cuddle on the sofa to watch TV, and spoon in bed with her just before falling asleep. It pleases me to awaken in the morning to her smile and kisses. I delight in stroking and rubbing her back to get her up. I love to smell her clean body after a shower. I pleasure in the tenderness of her hugs and caresses.

"I am deeply touched by the thoughtful things she does for me and the tender mercies she bestows on me. I find great comfort in her welcoming and supportive arms.

"I am pleasured most to hear her laugh with happiness." (Jo, age 37, 12-year couple)

STORY 5:

GAIL (age 39) & DONNA (age 36): 15 years together

Some couples report more troubles than others; Gail and Donna are one of those couples. During the interview we talked about what would seem to be more than one couple's share of problems: homophobia, dysfunctional families, incest, rape, a life-threatening car accident, alcoholism, and emotional abuse.

Gail and Donna are both well-educated and have a moderate income, which they share. They live in a semirural suburb outside Phoenix, Arizona. Gail is from a middle-class family; Donna's father was a skilled worker. Gail was brought up Catholic; Donna was raised in a fundamentalist Protestant family. Gail is an artist; Donna a pediatric nurse. They have been together fifteen years.

Gail and Donna do not have a history of prior relationships that would have allowed them to "practice" on someone else. Gail had only one significant relationship before Donna, a relationship with a woman that lasted two years. Gail is Donna's first and only significant relationship. Thus they have had to contend with all the problems of becoming lesbians and developing intimacy within the context of their relationship with each other. They got together when Gail was 24; Donna 21.

Here's the discussion among the three of us about this couple's struggle around roles and tasks:

> *Gail:* At one point we decided we were too much into roles, you know, like male-female roles. So we decided to switch those around.
>
> *Susan:* Just exchange them you mean?
>
> *Gail:* Yeah. So she would try to put oil in the car. She doesn't even pay attention to driving. How is she going to put oil in the car when she stops to get gas, which she never does? And I would actually do some cleaning, which I hate to do. We really tried to do this. I think it lasted two weeks. We played at it for maybe another six months, and finally decided to just be whoever it was we were.

Susan: And not worry about whether those tasks looked conventionally divided?

Donna: Right. Or whether they were actually balanced.

Gail: That was a big one: who's doing the most work?

Susan: So it wasn't the tasks themselves, it was the equality of . . .

Donna: And the value.

Gail: Always the same value!

Donna: Is taking the garbage out as valuable as unloading the dishwasher or folding the clothes or changing the oil or . . . ?

Gail: And we also have different time-lines. I'm happy to do laundry, but I don't do it until I need clean clothes. If there's a little stack of dirty clothes, Donna thinks it's time to do the laundry . . .

The judgments we made of each other. That was the real big thing. It's in the last couple of years that we've finally begun to quit making judgments. Not just on each other, but on ourselves and everything around us.

These partners have many differences (Gail: "We're gonna disagree — we're too different — we just aren't gonna agree.") not the least of which is a difference in emotional makeup:

Gail: I'm a real angry person. I have been my whole life. I'm less now than I ever have been, but I'm still way up there on the scale. Donna is not an angry person and is just now learning to be. So when we would fight, it was the style that came into conflict.

Gail's anger was often out of control, and her anger meshed perfectly with Donna's willingness to feel at fault. This wasn't just a matter of style; it was also a matter of chronic emotional damage.

Gail: I would blast everything. And Donna, if she were there, she would get it first and foremost. Then it would leak out to the other people who might have caused it. Or the anger would start with them, and I would finish it on her . . . When I was angry at something else, I'd go at her personally.

Donna: I responded very well, by taking all the responsibility; it was all my fault. I did that for years and years and years. It was a behavior that I knew. I knew how to be wrong.

Susan: From your family, you mean, you already knew that?

Donna: Yeah. And how to turn over the righteousness to someone else. How to let someone else be the authority. Because then I didn't have any power. I could be the victim and just give it all up and not even accept that I felt bad about myself. It was just that I was obviously wrong; it was my fault.

So when I got really tired of that — it took me years to get tired of that and identify that I was really tired of it — that's when we went into our most recent tailspin.

Susan: That's real interesting. It's like the system worked in its own sick way as long as you, Gail, were willing to dish it out, and you, Donna, were willing to take it on. But something happened. . . .

Gail: Well, I started changing. About four years ago all this counseling started to kick in, and I made major changes.

Gail and Donna have been helped hugely by individual and couples therapy. Gail recognizes that: "I do just get crazy sometimes." Elsewhere in the interview she explained a period in their lives with, "I was insane. I mean, I play with the edge a lot. I was way, way gone." She has also had her problems with alcohol, but is not drinking now.

Gail says therapy is the third most significant reason she and Donna have stayed together: "Number 3: Large quantities of good counseling." At various times in their relationship, and for years at a time, they have each done individual counseling as well as couples counseling together. It is not only a reason they are together but probably the reason they can be so articulate about their problems and the solutions they've found.

Their early therapy, about ten years ago, gave them some crucial communication skills. More recently they are struggling with the matter of change.

Gail: I quit teaching because I didn't want to be a closet lesbian any more; if I couldn't be who I was, I wasn't going to do it. I went through a whole series of changes.

Usually Donna is the one that does the changing first and pulls me along. Well, this time I changed. So then she started to change, but it wasn't in the ways I wanted. She was changing in the ways *she* wanted. Well! (Laughter)

Unfortunately she picked changes that made her emphasize more the parts of herself that I didn't like. Then I had one of my crazy periods, and I said, "I'll give you so long to change. At the end of that I'll decide whether I can live with that person or not."

So that's where we are right now. And the changes I'm seeing now are the ones that I like and that are more what I wanted. So it looks like it's going to work out okay. But neither one of us are the people we were two years ago. I never would have believed that this person is the same one that I got involved with at the beginning.

Donna: I think the same for me; Gail is making the changes that I've been waiting for.

Gail talked about the stages she's gone through in her growing acceptance of Donna's changes.

Gail: Several years ago it would have been "You can be that way, but I'll find a way to get you." It shifted from that to: "You can be that way but I think you're wrong, and I can always just leave."

Susan: You mean, "You can be that way if you want to be alone."

Gail: Yes. Then, "You can be that way, but I'll have to figure out what to do about it, how to live and not be upset about it." And now, finally, I think I'm coming to, "You can be that way."

Not every day. I can't feel that way every day, but more and more days, it's getting to, "You can just be that way."

I asked,

Susan: What's the impact of all this stuff on your sex life? Where are you with that?

Gail: I think nowhere.

Susan: You mean it's nonexistent?

Gail: It's hard to say yes to that. The first time I went to counseling it was about our sex life, and we ended up with all this other stuff. Our counselor basically said, "You're not going to get near sexual problems until you can take care of this other stuff." Like communicating, she meant.

Now sex has been on-line with our present counselor for at least a year, and all the other stuff keeps coming up. We keep clearing it out, and we're ready to deal with sex, and then Christmas came up, and . . .

Donna: Gail's crazies came up, and. . . . So we managed to find a variety of things to work on instead.

Gail: There's a lot of hugging, and periodically we do attempt sex, but I'd say it is without question the weakest spot. And so far we have not found a way to get through it.

Donna has a history of rape, by both men and women, and emotional incest, i.e., non-physical sexual abusiveness within her family. Donna: "I can identify how all those things affected me, but I don't know what I want to do about it."

Our discussion of the history of Donna's sexual abuse, both physical and emotional, leads us back to her relationship with Gail:

Gail: I think I used to emotionally abuse Donna through the anger.

Susan: Which you, Donna, would put up with by taking responsibility for it, and all that.

Donna: Yeah. And by trying and trying and trying and trying and being wrong forever. If I knew I was going to be wrong making dinner, I was certainly going to be wrong making love.

A little later,

Donna: We have said that what we do want is
a much more active sex life.

Gail: We've been saying that for years.

Gail has always threatened Donna with leaving.
She was far more reluctant to commit herself at the
beginning of their relationship, and she is always
careful to maintain escape routes in her mind. When
I ask in the questionnaire "What is your most honest
estimate of the likelihood that your relationship will
last?" almost everyone in the long-term couple says,
as Donna did, "My relationship will last forever."
Gail said, "I honestly don't have any idea," and
added, "But since we made it through this last crisis,
maybe for a long time."

Donna has felt firmly committed from the
beginning.

Donna: It feels to me like something I have no
control over. It's at a much deeper soul
level. I would say we are soul-bonded. I
believe that we've been together in many,
many, many other lifetimes. I have a
knowing inside myself that we'll be
rocking-chair people together. And I knew
that the day I met Gail. I just *know* that.
There's no question in my mind that you
would ever move out . . .

Gail: You've never believed that I would.

Donna: No. Or that I would leave you. I've
never believed that. She was the only
"real" person I was ever attracted to, what

I define as real. When I saw Gail I thought, that's the real thing. That's really what fits. So I don't know what that thread is that holds us together, except for me it's the real thing.

Gail: We're very good for each other. We've forced each other to grow; sometimes we've helped each other to grow. There's something underneath that every time everything else is smashed away, there's still that thread.

It takes a lot of different forms. I think that just a basic love for each other is the bottom. But I don't think that's enough by itself. There's some other thread with that. So every time we get into these crisis situations, that bottom line is still strong enough that we can't quite pull it apart and separate . . .

Maybe it's something inside that says, ultimately she's good for me. Like a survival instinct . . . Some sort of survival instinct combined with love.

. . . But there sure has been a lot of pain. A tremendous amount of pain.

On her questionnaire Gail wistfully sums up how hard the struggle has been. When asked, "Is there anything else you'd like to share with me?" she says, "I still don't understand why it can't be easy."

Chapter 5
Problems

I am cautious about making generalizations based on this study, but this is one I feel confident about: I believe couples who stay together do not have fewer or less serious problems than couples who break up. The lesbians who have maintained their relationships for ten years or more — the women in this study — have done so despite problems which would have been cause for the dissolution of other relationships. This is the chapter where we look at some of those problems and the adaptations these women have made, or the solutions they have found, that allow their relationships to continue.

Thinking About Breaking Up

This is how I phrased a question about breaking up: "During the course of many relationships, there are times when dissolving the relationship becomes a possibility. What were those times in the history of your relationship? And why *didn't* you break up when you might have?"

Fourteen percent of the couples have never considered a breakup: "I don't believe there was ever a time when our relationship was in trouble." (Mary, age 65, 39-year couple) But 12 percent actually have broken up for some period of time. I defined a breakup as a separation between the two women without any assumption on the part of at least one of the women that they would reunite. Table 5.1 shows the distribution of responses for the couples who answered this question.

Of the eleven couples who broke up, one had two separations totaling seven years out of an eighteen-year relationship. This couple has a complicated history. Joanna and Janice got together around 1970 when Janice was still married. They maintained the relationship as a triangle with Janice's husband while all three of Janice's children were born.

"There were several times when Joanna and I tried to separate due to my marriage.

206

TABLE 5.1 HOW MANY COUPLES HAVE CONSIDERED BREAKING UP?

Have you considered breaking up?	Number of couples	Percent of couples
No, never considered it	13	14.0
Partners disagree	7	7.5
Yes, we've considered it but didn't break up	62	66.7
Yes, we considered it, and did break up for a time	11	11.8
Totals	93*	100.0

*Number of couples who responded to this question.

These never worked because the marriage was so rocky." (Janice, age 42)

"When we first started living together, it was a three-way arrangement; me, my partner, and her husband. After her second child was born, we decided to live apart to see if her marriage could 'take over.' But it didn't. So we re-connected immediately after her third child. (This was a separation of about two years.)

"Our second breakup was because she had a relationship going on the side with her boss, and I finally felt cut out. So I did cut out. (This separation lasted five years.)

"So, when things get really bad, I leave. I will not stay in any relationship that has ended." (Joanna, age 58)

Clearly, something compelling kept these women coming back to each other. Joanna:

"We have experienced living alone, living with someone else whom we loved at the time, and living with someone whom we 'settled for' rather than live alone. We've had it all and know better what we want now.

"There really is a powerful connection between us that seems to be stronger than we are. No matter what happens to us, when the dust settles, we really want to be together."

More typical of the eleven breakups, however, is the shortest, which lasted about two months. The couple has been together twelve years.

"We did separate for a short time early in our relationship when my partner was unfaithful. However, we resolved the issue and decided not to make the separation permanent.

"Also, my partner is an alcoholic. She has been sober for two years now. As her drinking increased from when we first began our relationship, there were several times I considered leaving because of this. I feel that if she had not stopped drinking two years ago, I would have left eventually.

"I guess the reason I never left her is because I had come to realize that alcoholism is a disease. And I always hoped that through my encouragement and support, she would find the strength to enter treatment. She did."
(Pam, age 41)

Not many couples voluntarily mentioned alcohol as a problem, but I am struck with how many did so among the couples who have broken up for a time. (This study did not specifically ask about alcohol or drug problems.) All five of the couples who broke up for a year or more mention problems with alcohol. Of the six couples who broke up for less than one year, two mention alcohol. This means seven of the eleven couples who broke up had such problems.

A couple with alcohol and drug problems who considered breaking up, but didn't, explain why:

"After I chose sobriety, I stated that something needed to change in my partner's use of substances or I would have to leave. She chose sobriety." (Vivian, age 47, 10-year couple)

"My partner sobered up about three years into our relationship. I continued to use alcohol and drugs for another year, and only sobered up when my partner threatened to leave." (Susie, Vivian's partner, age 34)

The principal reason these women gave for having considered breaking up is conflict over outside relationships: affairs, interest in another woman, non-monogamy issues, triangles, etc. The second most frequently cited reason is psychological characteristics or behaviors of the woman herself or her partner. Table 5.2 shows the reasons women in long-term couples considered breaking up.

Here are some of the reasons these women

TABLE 5.2 REASONS FOR CONSIDERING A BREAKUP

Reason first mentioned	Number of women	Percent of women
Have never considered breaking up	36	18.2
Other (not classifiable in another category)	47	23.7
Affairs, interest in another woman, non-monogamy issues, triangles, etc.	45	22.7
Psychological characteristics/behaviors of self or partner (e.g., depression)	24	12.1
Children, stress of some aspect	9	4.5
Other relatives, often mothers	7	3.5
Job or school stress/dissatisfaction; change in jobs	6	3.0
Moving, relocation, geographical separation	5	2.5
Alcohol, drug problems	5	2.5
Attempt to save (heterosexual) marriage	5	2.5
Communication problems, unspecified about what	4	2.0
Sexual incompatibility; other sex problems	2	1.0
Not sure about being a lesbian	2	1.0
Money	1	0.5
Total	198*	100.0

*Number of women who responded to this question.

considered breaking up, and their analysis of why they chose not to.

Reason 1: Affairs, Interest in Other Women, etc.

"During the third year I had an affair,

which was out in the open. I think, whether I realized it or not, I was testing my commitment to Carol. I picked someone who was very different from her and had many of the qualities I felt Carol lacked and I needed. The affair didn't last long (less than two months).

"Simply put, I liked Carol better! But really what I mean is, it really clarified to me why Carol was so important to me and what I was getting from her that I truly did not want to lose." (Esther, age 42, 11-year couple)

"Four years into the relationship (of nineteen years) I became interested in someone else. It coincided with the purchase of our first home, which may have been a time of questioning what we had done.

"We discussed what had happened openly, and my partner gave me space to sort things out." (Lori, age 41)

"We were both having an affair with other women. We stayed together because we recognized the core reasons for the behaviors and knew we were running away from commitment to each other out of fear." (Angela, age 42, 11-year couple)

All three of these couples sound as if the experience with affairs left them wiser and more committed. That is not every couple's experience. Some affairs leave scars.

"During the fifth year, I became attracted to someone else, and considered breaking off the relationship. When things hit a critical point, I was forced to make a choice and discovered that I was unwilling to give up Jill. . . .

"After we survived the near break, it took a long time for Jill to trust me and for me to trust myself." (Cornelia, age 47, 17-year couple)

"The principal result of the extra-marital affair of my partner was the loss of true sexual intimacy between us. This has been touched on verbally sometimes, but has never been really resolved." (Victoria, age 70, 31-year couple. This couple has not been sexual for ten years).

Several of these women say or imply that their affairs were motivated by something other than sheer sexual or emotional interest in someone else ("testing my commitment," "questioning buying a house together," "running away from commitment out of fear"), i.e., the affair had to do with their couple relationship as much as it did with the other woman or man. These are, of course, analyses long after the fact, and often with the intervening interpretations of therapy. Nonetheless, we should be wary that what may feel at the time like passion for another, may instead be a red flag warning us of trouble in our relationship.

These attractions can, of course, be contained. Here's the advice of a woman in a fifteen-year couple:

"Realize that being attracted to someone doesn't mean you're in love or that you have to act on it. Realize that there are probably many different women out there that you could be attracted to and even live with, but you don't need to hop from relationship to relationship to find the perfect one; you have to build it." (Mary, age 36)

Reason 2: Psychological Characteristics/Behaviors of Self or Partner

"When my partner was very depressed for a long time and counselling didn't seem to help, I felt like number ten on her priority list, and separated.

"It was a good move. She seemed to come out of the depression. I/we really wanted our relationship to work. We had lots of family and friend support to hang in there (My parents love my partner.)" (Corinne, age 37, 12-year couple)

"Within the past few years, a bout with severe depression and boredom in our relationship threatened it. Rather than give up, we decided to work to rejuvenate our relationship. We have both benefitted from therapy, both as individuals and as a couple.

"I believe our ability to communicate and problem solve, as well as trust in each other kept us going." (Stella, age 36, 10-year couple)

Reason 3: Stress of Children

"My children have been a problem between us. Although two of my daughters have a good relationship with my lover now, the third is estranged from her. This has caused much heartbreak and anger on my part." (Shara, age 48, 13-year couple)

"She had young children (ages 10 and 12), and in the beginning the living situation seemed intolerable to me at times.
"But *she* never wavered, so that kept me hanging in." (Esther, age 64, 19-year couple)

Reason 4: Relatives

"My partner's mother lives with us and has for the last ten years. She's a difficult woman, and I feel is not really happy with me. My partner is in the middle. Sometimes I've felt like I'd be better off out of it.
"BUT LOVE CONQUERS. I do not want to live the rest of my life without my partner." (Elena, age 55, 19-year couple)

When these women reflect on the reasons they thought about breaking up, they are talking — most of them — about the past. They are talking about crises, traumas that they can isolate in time, that flared up, were dealt with, and then died down. When I ask about problems in a different way, about these couples' biggest source of problems, they are talking about issues that bother them now, perhaps chronic issues.

Biggest Source of Current Problems

The open-ended question I asked was: "What would you say is the single biggest source of problems for you and your partner in your relationship?" Table 5.3 shows the responses.

TABLE 5.3 BIGGEST SOURCE OF PROBLEMS

Nature of problem	Number of women	Percent of women
Some personality characteristic of self or partner	39	20.0
Money, especially the lack thereof	31	15.8
Sex	24	12.2
Time, not enough to spend together	16	8.2
Work, some aspect	14	7.1
Communication, misunderstandings	12	6.1
Relatives	11	5.6
Power differences between partners	8	4.1
Other	41	20.9
Total	196*	100.0

*Number of women who responded to this question.

Personality Characteristics

The problem many lesbians in long-term couples identify as their biggest source of problems are personality characteristics of themselves or their partners.

Remember those trifling but slightly obnoxious quirks of your new love's psychological makeup, those things you knew would disappear with time? Well, here they are, at least ten years later, still causing difficulties between you. Here are some examples of what these women cite as the biggest source of problems when "personalities" are involved.

"My partner's critical attitude about everything, including me, so I feel on the defensive, but mostly about little things. She has a tendency to be impatient with others' failings, but has excuses for her own. She's a born manager, and sometimes it's hard to acquiesce to her tendency to want to manage me as well as other things/people." (Victoria, age 70, 31-year couple)

Often the women describe their own personality "defect" rather than their partners'.

"My anger behavior." (Sally, age 37, 12-year couple)
My bullheadedness." (Jessica, Sally's partner, age 39)

It is extremely common for the lesbians in long-term couples to report a difference of temperament where one partner is quieter, slower, and uncomfortable with anger while the other is more verbal, fast-paced, and explosive. In fact, the combination is so common — more than half the couples report these differences — that I am tempted to argue that we often seek someone to complement our otherwise too introverted or too extroverted personality. While it may be common, however, this temperamental difference often causes difficulties; the balance achieved is not an easy one.

"I am quick to anger and easy to offend. My partner is slow to anger, and does not become insulted easily. When I am angry, I am direct, verbally aggressive, and confrontative. My partner is indirect, and more passive-aggressive about her anger. When we are faced with a tense situation, she feels that my behavior is rude; I see hers as indifferent." (Natasha, age 44, 12-year couple)

"The single biggest source of problems for myself and my partner in our relationship is our individual temperament styles. We may have similar goals, but each of us have different priorities for goal achievement. I work quickly; she, slowly, methodically, and thoroughly. I am intuitively creative; she wants the facts and the directions so things are done right. I see the big picture; she, the individual parts. I am likely to make snap decisions; she wants to study all possibilities. I am constantly doing activities (to the point of compulsiveness); she is slow to get motivated and enjoys relaxing. These are sources of irritation." (Monica, age 37, 12-year couple)

Such differences of temperament may make for a good balance if we think of the couple as an entity in itself. But it is clear that each partner often experiences the difference as a chronic source of difficulty.

Money

The second most often cited source of problems is money, most often the lack of it.

"We agree on how to spend money, but the lack of it causes anxiety and often produces stress in other areas of our lives." (Kathy, age 33, 14-year couple)

Sometimes, though, the problem has more to do with attitudes toward money, attitudes which may cause conflict or at least discomfort for the couple. Lauren and Beverly are a well-to-do couple who've been together thirteen years. Lauren is 47 and makes more than $50,000 per year in a sales occupation. Beverly is 58 and earns less than half what Lauren does. At this point in the interview we'd discussed several problems they had resolved without too much difficulty. Beverly is outside having a cigarette, but listening to this interchange and nodding her agreement.

Susan: All this sounds very easy. Tell me about something that hasn't been so easy.

Lauren: Well, the money hasn't been completely easy. Beverly sometimes doesn't feel good about not having as much income as I do. She is not comfortable unless she feels as though she's contributing, and even when she is working fulltime, which she hasn't been for a while, there's still a little bit of uneasiness that I don't feel at all.

It has never bothered me that she never made as much money. Very few women make as much money as I do. I don't have any resentment at all. There's no feeling that "I'm contributing more than you, therefore I should get more of something." I've never felt that way.

But she has felt somewhat insecure about it, and there's nothing I can do. That's her problem that she has to resolve or live with or whatever. I can't help her with that.

Susan: Do you talk about it?

Lauren: We do, we do, and there's nothing that we can resolve. She has to come to some conclusion of her own, which I don't believe she ever really has. I don't think she ever will.

Susan: I think that's an interesting thing about long relationships, sometimes there are issues that just aren't resolvable . . .

Lauren: Yeah. You just have to learn to live with them.

Beverly returns to the table.

> *Susan:* We were talking about the income discrepancy, is that making you feel uncomfortable?
>
> *Beverly:* Yeah, yeah. Though I've adapted a great deal, haven't I?
>
> *Lauren:* Well, from time to time it still gets you.
>
> *Beverly:* That's true, it does.
>
> *Lauren:* I think it probably has to do with feeling insecure about other things. It doesn't bother you all the time.
>
> *Beverly:* Right. It peaks only at certain times.

Sex

The third most often experienced problems center around sex. An entire chapter has been devoted to the issue of sexuality in long-term couples. Here I would like to describe how one couple has experienced a link between problems with sexuality and problems with communication. The differences of temperament are apparent too.

Esme and Valerie are in their early to mid-60s. They both work in academic environments, and have been together eighteen years.

> *Susan:* One of the things you both talk about in the questionnaire is communication and how important that is. When you say "communication," what do you mean by that?

Esme: I probably have a more strident style than Valerie was used to in her childhood. Things that I say she can take as threatening. I don't mean it that way. I have a great curiosity to find out about things, to learn about things, and I'm liable to push really hard for this. Valerie immediately thinks she's being attacked and backs off. I think she's being defensive . . . we just aren't firing together.

Valerie: I think we used to have just absolutely terrific communication. Things were funny when they were meant to be funny, but now we're so likely to take offense somehow. I think our communication has gone downhill.

Susan: Why do you think that?

Valerie: I think communication became more difficult as we grew apart physically. We had to make up for it with all this therapy to really understand each other.

Esme and Valerie have not been sexual with each other in the past year. They recount some physical and stress-related problems that contributed to their distance. But they come back to how these things impacted their sexual life.

Esme: I think our physical separation did create problems. Valerie was uptight with her work, and I was learning something new in my job. The tensions were such that we really physically did not reach for each other. Or if we did, they were at disparate times, so that each one of us probably felt we were being rejected. And it set up a pattern.

Susan: A pattern that persists?

Esme: I think it's one we're trying to break.

Susan: What effect do you think that's had on your relationship as a whole?

Valerie: I think it's had a vast effect. I think that's the seed of all this stuff about communication.

Susan: What do you think the effect is?

Valerie: The communication became different. It became more literal, more tight, more apt to be misinterpreted, more apt to be defensive. Just more difficult.

Esme: I think the difference is that making love, a sharing of the physical, loosens up the intellectual and the ability to talk.

Valerie: Absolutely, absolutely. It builds trust.

Problem Couples

Over the months that I reflected on these women's questionnaires and interviews, I found myself thinking of some of the couples as "problem couples," relationships that are significantly more troubled than the others. (These are simply my impressions, not a clinical diagnosis.)

I eventually came to see 15 of the 108 couples as "problem couples." I would be reading along in a couple's questionnaire, and gradually begin to feel uneasy. I'd come upon some major discrepancy of perception between the partners, coupled with accounts of lingering problems with alcohol, or references to physical abuse, or expressions of what seemed like severe depression. It wasn't any one thing that would make me wary, but the combination: troubled sex plus lack of money plus alcohol abuse plus very different perceptions. Let me give you the features I finally concluded were alerting me to what I thought of as serious problems, with some examples of each. Remember, though, that more than one of these problems needs to be present.

Lack of communication/different perceptions of the relationship/denial: A couple together thirteen years disagrees about whether they are lovers. Claire, age 41, says she does not consider them lovers and that they haven't made love in at least the last year; her partner Naomi, age 32, says they make love a few times a year and that she is very satisfied with their sexual relationship. They also do not agree — and do not know they disagree — about monogamy. Claire says, "We have allowed each other to have affairs and I think the relationship suffers if either one feels 'smothered.' " Naomi says they have discussed outside relationships and agreed that under no circumstances are they all right.

Power in this relationship is very skewed, and there is a problem with alcohol, as well as too little money.

In another couple (twelve years together), the mother of two children is eloquent about her close family: "totally beautiful family togetherness." Her partner talks of the family relationships in terms of: "jealousy," "embarrassment," "resentment," "serious conflicts."

There is a history of physical abuse, and problems

223

with alcohol. Also too little money and some serious mental illness, I suspect.

Physical abuse: A twenty-six-year couple handles conflict like this:

> "We yell at each other until someone gives way! We used to occasionally have physical fights. (I would say she escalated to this level. She is more emotional; I am more rational. We each drive the other nuts.)"

This couple is still struggling with issues of equality. ("We both secretly want to be on top rather than equal, so battle it out.") They fight "fairly" or "very" frequently.

They give as reasons for staying together "inertia" and "We wouldn't know how to split up the cats."

Depression/resignation: Sometimes the signs of depression or hopelessness are subtle but painfully honest:

> "Sometimes I feel like I am changing and this may affect our relationship. I'm not sure how. Probably just my insecurity in myself: She loves me more than I love me.
>
> "Formerly I stayed in this relationship because I was more dependent; I felt I would be lost without my partner. Now I stay because I owe it to her; I promised, and I still love her." (Jane, age 39, 12-year couple)

Jane and her partner agree their relationship is unequal.

Depression may be related to ill health. One woman, Suzette, (age 54, 11-year couple) is in remission from a recent cancer, and her questionnaire reads like someone who is very depressed.

She's not happy with her and her partner's sex life, although they make love two to three times per month: "My expectations for exciting sex have changed considerably. I am resigned." Responding to the questions about longevity, she says, "I honestly don't have any idea how long my relationship will last," and "I never expected it to last this long."

She says her partner has more power and makes more important decisions. She sounds tired: "We talk about whatever conflict we may be having. Often I get worn down and give up."

Her partner Janice, age 39, is coping bravely:

"Since my partner's cancer, I have very quickly learned to appreciate every day, even the bad ones in a strange way. Life-threatening illnesses have a way of adjusting priorities and the things we appreciate."

Severe sexual problems: A seventeen-year couple disagrees about whether or not they consider themselves lovers and about monogamy. One of the women is very unhappy with what she perceives as the lack of sex in their lives:

"I feel very frustrated, ugly, and unhappy, and would like to find a solution.

"I sometimes feel that I should seek professional help to learn how better to cope

with the absence of sex in our relationship,
but it is so very painful that I don't know if I
would have the ability to talk rationally."
(Helen, age 46)

Asked her best estimate of how long her
relationship will last, Helen says: "My relationship
will last for a while."

Helen's partner Nancy, age 59, seems completely
unaware of Helen's misery. She says they make love
once every few months, though she is only moderately
satisfied with their sex life. She says, "My
relationship will last forever."

A severe health problem is relevant to this
relationship. And this couple does not talk about
their problems with each other; it's become too
painful.

In fact, I would say that when couples stop
talking about their problems with each other, the
relationship is in serious trouble. Not that they may
break up — you remember that all the "problem
couples" are still together, one for twenty-six years —
but that they are no longer able to intervene in their
problems. They probably cannot solve anything until
they begin to talk again.

Solutions: Communication

Many of the themes I want to talk about as
solutions are represented in the following account
from a ten-year couple: the loss of communication and
its renewal; the use of therapy; and an eventual

realization of one's own responsibility for what happens in our lives. Here is one partner's description, a model of brevity.

"We stopped talking. I was dissatisfied with my work, became withdrawn, entered therapy, met someone else, became diverted by a brief infatuation. My partner then started coming for therapy, and we worked it out." (Leila, age 41, 10-year couple)

Here is the longer version of the same story from Ann, age 46, Leila's partner.

"For various reasons we both 'shut down' almost entirely and stopped talking to each other. (This resulted from historical as well as situational factors in both our lives and in our life together.)

"My partner started therapy and shortly thereafter was attracted to someone else. I panicked and wanted to run away, but also wanted to stop running away (both literally and metaphorically), so I went into individual therapy also. Eventually we did some therapeutic work together and learned to start talking again and to process stuff together.

"This work was extremely helpful, but what saved our relationship, I think, is that we both learned, through our individual work, to take responsibility for our own lives and to work out our own 'histories' and developmental problems. We helped each other do that through the strength and inherent 'goodness' of our relationship.

"So, because there was a whole lot of growing (hers, mine, ours) going on, we didn't break up when we might have. We all got better!"

Communication is a key to problem-solving. The problems of temperament women report always have a communication component that is part of the difficulty: "direct and verbally aggressive" versus "indirect and passive/aggressive." A 33-year partner says her biggest source of problems is:

"Wishing sometimes my partner was more outspoken and honestly expressed how she feels. She 'clams up' and doesn't confront the problem. I'm the opposite and probably overexpress myself at times, then give up. So we don't resolve the problem at that time." (Valerie, age 64)

Communication is necessary; we must learn to talk with each other despite these style differences. I asked, "How do you deal with conflicts that arise between you? Please describe briefly what you typically do when you have a conflict?" The answers are descriptions of these couples' communication under stress.

"Worst case: I discuss it calmly, maybe get accusatory. She defends, gets mad, we scream, take space, forget it.

"Best case: We calmly discuss." (12-year couple)

"We try to talk over our feelings and what we ought to do. Each person gets to say everything she wants to say. We don't call each other names or be abusive, but we're not above yelling at each other. Usually we get tired of being mad and either someone gives in or we compromise. We have a rule about not going to bed angry, which sometimes requires late hours." (15-year couple)

"We talk about it, listening to each other, ideally without becoming defensive and interrupting. We try to understand each other's point of view, not having to be right, and the other wrong. Also, we let each other have "Her Day." We take turns having "Our Day," where we get to have our way that day, within reason." (12-year couple)

"I try to talk about whatever it is right then, but often (because of children) we need to schedule a time to have a discussion. This works, as it gives me time to cool down, and my partner time to open up and be less intimidated by my anger." (14-year couple)

Some women readily admit they are not good at communication under conflict conditions.

"We're getting better, but each of us still

tends to sit on a problem until it's too big to ignore. I especially don't always realize I'm upset at first. Eventually we talk it out and wonder why we didn't do it sooner." (15-year couple)

Many of the women — like this twenty-nine-year couple — don't like conflict either.

"I feel awful, sometimes misunderstood that it had to happen, become a conflict." (Anne, age 63)

"I scold. She blames. I get furious. She weeps. Silence. Within the hour we calm down, forgive and console. It just happens. Later we hug and kiss. We both feel guilty and sorry for the other." (Lillian, age 66)

Of course different issues have different potentials for volatility. It's easier to communicate about some things than others. Here's how one woman details the differences (she's responding to a question about certain types of problems and how frequently they're an issue):

"With issues that are rarely a problem (like for us chores or money), we usually discuss the conflict reasonably and arrive at a consensus decision.
"With those that are sometimes a problem (like friends or relatives or sexual differences), it takes us longer and we usually have to

recognize differences in personal values and reach a compromise.

"If it's an issue that is frequently a problem (children, for us), we have ongoing struggles, but have been able to resolve specific incidents with at least an ability for both of us to live with it." (Joan, age 41, 17-year couple)

This discussion of how the women communicate about different problems using different techniques and achieving different results brings up an issue I think we ignore. When we promote good communication we are advocating something that is not for the faint of heart. Communication involves not only *how* something is said but *what* is said. It's about technique and content both.

I suspect that what often stymies good communication is not that we don't know how to say what we want to say, but that we're afraid to say it. It's the content that is too frightening, not the approach. We're afraid that what we need to say won't be heard openly, will make our partner angry, will "cause trouble;" we're afraid of the consequences of what we need to say.

Some couples are comfortable with communicating about difficult things.

"Each person gets to have her say. We can get mad. We can cry. If it's something that we can negotiate about, we try to. Some things are never truly 'solved,' we just have to accept our differences and go on. Usually conflict (even an unresolved one) makes us feel closer." (Jolie, age 42, 11-year couple)

231

This is the key, is it not? Communication, especially about difficult things, helps us feel closer. It is, most clearly, what I believe these women mean when they say you have to "work" on your relationship; they mean you have to talk . . . and listen.

Solutions: Therapy

Half the couples attest to the help they've received from therapists, and more might have done so had I asked specifically for this information. Clearly, our couple relationships benefit greatly from good therapy.

Therapy helps immensely with techniques for good communication, especially under combat conditions.

> "Now we discuss problems until we reach an even place. What used to take weeks can now be done in less than an hour. Techniques learned at counseling have helped a lot." (Gail, age 39, 15-year couple)

> "When I was in graduate school, we began to communicate less, to shut down, each in her own way. Twice we went together to see counselors (two different periods of time, two different therapists). Both times, I feel we were helped in our communication with each other." (Cora, age 41, 15-year couple)

> "Between years five and six our relationship was tested by my partner getting

involved with another woman. After discussion she was willing to go to counseling and decided that our relationship was more important. We learned steps to maintain and enrich what we had." (Franny, age 38, 13-year couple)

Therapy can also help with the content: What are you trying to say to your partner? Is it about this particular situation or about something else? Is it about the present or something in your past? What is the truth for you here?

A woman in a ten-year relationship talks about this aspect of therapy when she's describing her and her partner's conflict style:

"We exchange nasty words. Anymore (after our therapy training) this is a clue to us to start figuring out what's wrong, what's hurting, what's triggering defensiveness. We seem to reach a resolution now more predictably, and/or recognize when one of us is just cranky and needing to rant and rave a little. We don't take it so personally as we used to." (Mary, age 39)

Others agree that therapy helped them redefine, understand, and thus resolve crises in their relationship.

"My partner had an affair. We stayed together partially because she agreed immediately to end it, and because a therapist helped us realize it was the stress of our living

233

situation as much as anything that motivated it." (Kathleen, age 39, 13-year couple)

"I was unable to make a 100 percent commitment until four years into our relationship because I was questioning my sexuality and whether I wanted children and a traditional family. I 'dated' a man for one or two months and started therapy. In therapy I realized my pain was around disappointing my family by being gay, not being gay itself.

"I acknowledged my happiness and emotional and sexual satisfaction with Martha and made a lifelong commitment." (Bonnie, age 36, 10-year couple)

The experience of therapy is, of course, not much easier than the experience of long-term coupledom. With both, you need to tell the painful truths about yourself to another person and, worse yet, to yourself.

"I became emotionally involved with a man at work and lied to my partner about it. We came very close to breaking up, but just weren't willing to give each other up! Instead we faced the next worst possible thing: working through all that shit!

"We made a commitment to do it, and, with the help of some good counselors, did it." (Jan, age 33, 11-year couple)

Jan gives advice many of the couples would second:

"Being in a couple takes a lot of very hard work, the hardest work you'll ever do! If you want it, you have to make it a priority and work for it. If you love each other enough, it is worth it to work through the hard times.

"Use counseling."

Solutions: Time Passes

One of the huge advantages of a long-term relationship is that, by definition, time is on your side. Some problems disappear with time: children grow up and move away; illnesses heal; equality issues even out; keeping track becomes too difficult and time-consuming and silly; we learn to see the bigger picture once time has shown us a piece of it; we gradually adapt to each other's natures (Anna: "We've rubbed off the rough edges.").

And we heal from the wounds we have inflicted on each other.

"It is nice to realize how positive I feel about our relationship. I lost those feelings for several years. I felt betrayed (her partner had a secret affair), like I would never trust again or let myself find meaning in our relationship. Healing has indeed taken effect.

"I needed to learn some things, and we went about it the hard way, but we made it. It was so hard to lose respect for my partner. It was as if something died, but I realize I have regained those feelings. We have made mistakes and still have disagreements, but we have learned so much and loved so much that our relationship has remained intact.

"I thank the goddess for the chance to spend my life with my dearest friend and dearest love." (Sandra, age 32, 11-year couple)

Or at least we almost heal.

Frances: The love between us has been from the beginning the most profound thing that happened to either one of us. So anything else that's coming our way, it's just like water over the dam, without really affecting those feelings.

Ellen: The trust was damaged. (She's talking about her partner's infatuation and affair.)

Susan: When trust has gotten damaged, what have you done about that?

Ellen: Well, it's healed over, over time I think. But I still check, if things don't add up. Before, the trust used to be 100 percent. Now maybe it will max out at 98 percent.

Solutions: The Problem of Our Self

My therapist jokes — though I know it's not entirely a joke — that doing therapy with people younger than 40 is largely a waste of time. The reason is that when we're young, we keep seeking the solutions for our problems outside ourselves: if only we move on, if only we change partners, things will get better.

We may have to make several of these moves before we realize that the constant in our recurringly painful situations is us. To paraphrase Pogo: I have found the problem, and she is me. (Pogo said, "We have met the enemy and he is us.") It's at this point, when we begin to realize that the source of our problems is ourselves, that we can work effectively in therapy.

It's also at this point that we can begin to find solutions to the problems we have with our partners. A woman in a ten-year couple gives this advice:

"Don't try to change each other as persons. Learn to accommodate each other and, if necessary — and it probably is in most cases — each person should work to change herself in the ways she wants to change to become the person she wants to be.

"To be a healthy relationship, I think the relationship must support each partner as individuals. Don't blame your partner when things aren't the way you want them to be, take responsibility for 'allowing' them to be that way, or take responsibility for seeing that you get what you want, or working toward that." (Christie, age 46)

Notice here how Lillian, the 60-year-old partner in a thirty-one-year couple, shifts her attention from complaints she has about her partner to a recognition of her own responsibility. She starts by talking about her reaction to fights they have.

"I sometimes do sound sarcastic, or make a

really nasty remark. But I almost never turn it in my mind into a general anti-Victoria feeling. If I ever do wonder, 'Why am I staying?,' and I do, occasionally, I say to myself, 'My God, there isn't anybody as pleasing to be with as Victoria is.'

"And secondly, my good sense tells me that I would be lonely alone, and that there's nobody else that I would get mad at any less than Victoria.

"I mean, I know that these are really my own problems. They really are probably not Victoria's faults, they're my faults. So you can't escape that; that's you."

There is another side to all this. I don't want to be a Pollyanna about the business of accepting responsibility for "the problem of yourself" and imply that all will magically become wonderful once you change yourself (as if that were easy). I don't want us to uncritically adopt some chic idea that really contributes to our own victimization, to our believing that "it's all my fault." Sometimes characteristics of your partner or of the external situation can create a host of difficulties: she may have personal issues that seriously affect her ability to be in a couple. She may be alcoholic, or immature, or cruel, or crazy. In fact, it may not be possible to maintain your relationship with her, given the problems she poses.

But it remains true that you have the power to be the person you want to be, even faced with such difficulties. You can be balanced. You can avoid being an enabler, you can be grown-up, kind and reasonable. And you may decide you need to leave, that is your responsibility too.

Leaving may be the only solution. With all this talk of long-term relationships, I don't want to imply that you must stay put when to do so is simply too damaging to you or your partner. Sometimes getting out is the greatest kindness. What I want to point out is that, if the problem tags along with you because it *is* you, leaving will not be a solution.

STORY 6:

RENA (age 40) & MATTIE (age 33): 12 years together

Rena and Mattie have negotiated a lot of differences in their relationship. Rena is seven years older than Mattie. Rena is white and Polish, Mattie is black. Mattie is middle class, Rena working class. But they've shared a crucial similarity, their commitment to family. Rena: "It was really a value of both of us that we participate in our families."

Mattie's family of origin is in Missoula, Montana, where she and Rena have lived for more than twelve years. Rena's family is in the east. During the interview they told a lot of family stories.

Mattie: When I was a little kid — no older than my son here, maybe five or so — my grandmother said to me, "Never sleep with a woman, cause you'll never want to sleep with a man again." I remember consciously thinking, "Well, why bother sleeping with men, then? Why settle for anything less?"

Their families were stricken when they got together, but they have since rallied.

Mattie: I think it was very difficult for my mother just because another woman was closer to me than she was. She resented that.

Rena: Well, you'd been the head of the family for a long time . . . your mom was a single parent for a long time. . . .

Mattie: We were kinda close. Too close. I had already started making some boundaries between her and me, but once I got into this relationship, the boundaries became much more up-front instead of subtle ones. My mom had a hard time with that.

We talked about it over lunch one day with my sister. My mom said all these traditional things, "Oh, it's a phase, you'll grow out of it." "No, Mother, I won't grow out of it." "Well, maybe you had bad experiences with men." "No, Mother, I had very nice relationships with men." "Well, is it something I did wrong?" "No, Mother, there's nothing you did wrong. It's just the way I am."

"Well," my sister said, "I feel it's my Christian duty to tell you it's a sin." I said, "I don't think it's a sin." She said, "I've done my Christian duty. Now, what's for lunch?" And that's the last we ever discussed it.

My stepfather, who's a Baptist minister, said, "Are you sure that you made this decision and not somebody else?" He thought I was being co-opted by this white girl, right?

Susan: An older white woman.

Mattie: An older white woman, who does these things to young black girls for kicks.

Rena: It was a lotta kicks, I must admit!

Mattie: I said, "If she's doin' it for kicks, we're both having a great time!" I think that's the last he ever said.

Oh no, one more thing. He said, "Are you sure you know what you're doing?" I said, "Yes." He said, "Okay. Don't bring her to dinner." I said, "If she doesn't come to dinner, I'm not coming to dinner. You let Dan bring his girlfriend to dinner; you let Lora bring her husband to dinner. If Rena can't come, I won't come." He said, "So bring her. We'll make sure there's a place for her."

Rena: He's a practical man. Last year in California — Mattie's parents had moved to California — he introduced us all in

243

church. Except he forgot my name. He
called me "A dear, dear friend."

Mattie: You can't expect him to stand up in
the pulpit and say, "This is my
daughter-in-law." Although he did say,
"These are my grandsons," and there we
all stand, one son white, one son black.

A little later I brought the discussion back to how
Mattie had handled her stepfather saying she couldn't
bring Rena to dinner.

Susan: I wonder if sometimes our parents say
something rejecting or controlling in almost
a ritualized way, not knowing what will
happen, but some of us let them get away
with it. You came back at him right then,
instead of coming back at him five years
later, you know? I wonder if there's a lot
more we could do to control our parents
and their reactions if we were just stronger
or didn't take them so seriously.

Rena: Didn't take it like a kid.

Susan: Right.

Rena: Well, I think when you get married, or
have kids, you have to do that anyway; you
have to make your own rules.

Rena's relationship with her parents was more
strained. When she tried to tell her mother about her
and Mattie, five years into their relationship, her
mother said, "Why are you telling me this?"

Rena: "I thought maybe you'd like to know

me, Mom." Her whole response was, "Why would I want to know about your sex life?"

I never really told my dad. One time we took a walk, and he said, "When are you gonna find yourself a nice man?" I said, "I'm not. I'm committed to Mattie; we're gonna live together, you know." He said, "Yeah? Well, she's a nice girl." That was that.

Mattie's relationship with Rena's father was difficult, but she attacked the problem head-on.

Rena: My father's your basic bigot. I mean, Mattie's an exception, and he loves her son to death. But race was what he couldn't handle at first. It wasn't just being dykes; it was that she was black.

Mattie: He was okay. The first time he came out to visit us, he and I were going someplace, and he was gonna say something racist, but I said it first. So he proceeded to lecture me on why I shouldn't say things like that.

Then I told him that my father was upset that I was gonna live with a white woman. And he got real huffy and said, "My daughter's good enough to live with anybody!"

Rena: That was the end of that conversation.

Susan: Mattie, were your parents more upset about the lesbian part or the white part?

Mattie: I think they had a hard time at first with the multiracial aspect, but that kind of paled because I was with a woman. My mother said, "Who can think about that — that she's white — when we have this — that she's a woman — to figure out? The other is almost incidental."

Mattie and Rena each had a child, about seven years into their relationship. Rena became pregnant by artificial insemination. And a few months before she was due, Mattie's pregnant sister proposed that Mattie and Rena adopt her baby. They decided that, since they were prepared for one baby, they could handle two. The boys are now five years old.

> *Rena:* I told my mother I was gonna have a baby. She said, "How are you gonna raise a baby without a man?" I said, "I already talked with my brother and Mattie's brother, and they're willing to be involved, and, anyway, half the babies in the country are raised without men. My baby will be lucky to have two parents!"
>
> The relationship between me and my mom was so difficult, though, that I didn't ask her to come when the baby was born. I didn't want her to come. After that, she kind of cleaned up her act. I think she got the point that she could be part of this family or not, but my family was still here; it would go on without her. After that she started talking to me. It has taken some time, but I think we're okay now.

Rena and Mattie emphasized that family support

is reciprocal; ideally our families deserve our support as much as we deserve theirs.

> *Mattie:* It was important for my family that we be supportive of what they were doing as well. Like, if my father had something important going at church, he would call and ask us to come, both of us. It would be important to him that we were there.
> *Rena:* So we went.
> *Mattie:* And now my family would never dream of doing something without Rena there.
> *Rena:* If I didn't bring the macaroni salad, they'd be really mad.
> *Mattie:* Her job is to make macaroni salad.
> *Rena:* We're really institutionalized!
> *Mattie:* Her other job is to shut up about having to drink Kool-Aid.

Much of the interview was spent talking about differences between Rena and Mattie (race/culture, class, age: see Chapter 3), so it struck me as important that we talk about how they were managing to raise two children together. Rena was out of the room for this interchange.

> *Susan:* How do you agree on how to raise the kids? You have this major project that you are doing together.
> *Mattie:* We got a dog first. We thought if we could raise a puppy, we could raise a kid. If the dog didn't turn out too badly, then the kids might have a chance.
> Also, as social workers we had both

worked with other people's kids a long time before we got together, so we knew each other's parenting styles, and what each other's values were.

Susan: Are your parenting styles similar?

Mattie: Mostly. I'm probably the stricter of the two. And I have high expectations. I'm very rigid about the things my son needs to know in order to survive as a black male. And about what her son needs to know as a blond, blue-eyed, white male . . . there are some things he needs to know too.

Before we had kids we spent a lot of time talking about what was important, and what kinds of things we wanted them to know. We had this list of attributes for the ideal child. It was real funny. How would a child need to be in order to survive in this family?

Susan: Can you remember what some of those things were?

Mattie: You needed to like to talk, like to snuggle and be held, like to eat, and have a good sense of humor. If a kid could do those things, they were gonna make it with us. And the boys like to eat, like to snuggle, have a good sense of humor, and they're very articulate. I don't know if they came that way, or if we reinforced those things, but it's made for a great family!

The two boys were not the first creative product of this couple. Earlier in their relationship they had founded and run the women's bookstore in their

248

community, first out of their own basement, later in a separate space. Rena and Mattie have been central to the lesbian community in Missoula.

Susan: Tell me how the lesbian community has been supportive of your relationship, or not supportive.

Rena: I think they were really supportive of us as a couple because we started the bookstore. I was active in consciousness-raising groups, so a lot of lesbians who came out, came out in my groups. I got to be the mother there. We were very central to the community.

But, thinking before babies, there was the phase in the lesbian community about monogamy versus non-monogamy. Our community was really into recovery from every kind of dependency, substances or people, so anything you did was criticized for being co-dependent and enmeshed.

Mattie: When the issue was monogamy versus non-monogamy, women were really uptight that we were so monogamous. For awhile they would try to engage us in these political discussions; they would try to get us with "it's not politically correct." But they were talking to the wrong person. I haven't been politically correct my whole life, so fuck it. You know? Don't tell me how to be.

Rena: And it's hard to tell the women who started the feminist bookstore that they're not politically correct.

249

Mostly my friends were all laughing, "Thank heaven she finally got a lover."

Mattie: My straight black friends all dropped me.

Susan: Because?

Mattie: Because well-brought-up black girls aren't lesbians. It was the same message I got back in high school when I was an untraditional middle-class black girl. I wouldn't do things then — society-type things — like I was supposed to either; I got away with it because I was smart and I was nice.

Rena: The last friend dropped her because we were the only relationship she knew of that wasn't abusive that had been together more than three years.

Mattie: And we seemed to be happy. She dropped me because my relationship with Rena was good. Again, I wasn't doing it right. She and her friends were all in relationships where they got beat up all the time. They'd found these supposedly nice guys with good jobs, but it wasn't working. And mine was. She literally said, "I can't handle it, being friends with you."

Some of her friends were killed from abusive relationships, but I wasn't doing it right!

The lesbian community got used to Rena and Mattie being together and being monogamous.

250

Rena: And then we had boy babies. That wiped out half the community we knew.

Susan: Because of the babies, or because they were boys, or both?

Rena: Because of the boy babies. Our friend had a girl baby, and it didn't happen to her. But, although some lesbians dropped out, some were right with us too. They helped a lot! They were really supportive. And some of the people who dropped out . . .

Mattie: Came back around.

This past year has been hell for Rena and Mattie. Mattie: "I think we were as close to breaking up as we ever have come . . . I never want to live this year again; it felt like one damn crisis after another."

Rena changed jobs; then her father became very ill, and eventually died; her back went out and required surgery; she was stoned all the time on the medication; eventually she went back to work and got laid off, meaning Mattie had to find full-time work quick. (Mattie and Rena exchange years working and taking care of the kids.)

Rena and Mattie had planned to redo their kitchen, a creative project that would signal that normal times had returned.

Mattie: To me the kitchen was a symbol that life was gonna get better someday . . . and then Rena cancelled the kitchen. It was like she took away all my hope that life was ever gonna get normal. And I lost it. We were having these intense, screaming fights.

Susan: So how come you didn't break up in all of this?

Rena: Well, it would have been a *lot* of trouble! Just another trauma.

Mattie: Just another trauma.

Rena: Maybe I would have walked out, but I couldn't walk.

Mattie: I would have packed up, but my stuff was all over cause we were gonna get the kitchen redone.

Rena: And we do have two kids.

The stress of this time had a disastrous impact on Rena and Mattie's sexual life, normally a satisfying and important part of their relationship. They managed to hold themselves together in part by being with other lesbians.

Mattie: As soon as we could, we made an effort to go to community events so that we could remember, remember that we were lovers and that things could be good.

Rena: To get filled up. Because we couldn't fill each other up; we were just too exhausted.

Mattie: We just surrounded ourselves, immersed ourselves in lesbians. That really helped.

Rena: That's always what I need when I'm just feeling burned out. I have to go out and get some energy, you know? It's always fun to go out and watch the baby dykes. I admit voyeurism, I don't care!

Susan: They do have all that energy.

252

Rena: Did we look that glued together when we were first together?

Mattie: You know we didn't, because I have never been like that in public.

Rena: Well, I checked that out with a couple of people, Mattie, and they say we looked just as bad. Maybe even worse!

* * * * *

I asked Rena and Mattie their advice for lesbians who want to stay together. They said:

1. Communication: Mattie: "The best investment we ever made was a one-day workshop on communication, how to fight fair."
2. Liking to do things together: Rena: "We love to plan and do projects."
3. Therapy: Rena: "When you get in trouble, go see somebody."
4. Taking time together: Rena: "You have to go out and enjoy each other."
5. Rena: "And take care of yourselves."
6. Mattie: "And ignore the rules."

Chapter 6
Children, Family and Friends

No couple exists in a vacuum; there are always other people who play a significant role in any couple's existence. This chapter focuses on the supportive (and sometimes destructive) roles played by people who are important to long-term lesbian couples: parents, children, friends, the lesbian community, and the larger society.

Parents

There is an enormous variation in the kinds of relationships the women in long-term lesbian couples have with their parents. Here is an example. Loren, age 58, and Amy, age 54, have been together twenty-three years. Loren's mother has been extremely supportive of their relationship: Loren: "My mother adores Amy. She considers her another daughter." Amy's mother, in contrast, was, in the words of her daughter, a "cruel mother": Amy: "My mother was a serious problem to us for the first thirteen years. She died in 1979. Her jealousy and hatred for my mate made it difficult." Loren says, "When Amy's mother was alive, she hated me." Loren and Amy were and are still completely closeted

TABLE 6.1 HOW OPEN THE WOMEN ARE WITH THEIR MOTHERS

Degree of openness		Number of women	Percent of women
Very open: Response =	1	59	31.6
	2	23	12.3
	3	17	9.1
	4	6	3.2
	5	13	7.0
	6	1	0.5
	7	11	5.9
	8	6	3.2
Not at all open: R =	9	51	27.3
Total		187*	100.0

*Number of women who responded to this question.

TABLE 6.2 HOW OPEN THE WOMEN ARE WITH THEIR FATHERS

Degree of openness		Number of women	Percent of women
Very open: Response =	1	45	27.1
	2	15	9.0
	3	10	6.0
	4	6	3.6
	5	15	9.0
	6	0	0.0
	7	7	4.2
	8	8	4.8
Not at all open: R =	9	60	36.1
Total		166*	100.0

*Number of women who responded to this question.

with their parents, as they are with everyone except gay male and lesbian friends.

The lesbians in long-term couples differ a great deal in how they handle the problem of how open to be with their parents. I asked, "To what extent are yon open with the following people about your lesbian or gay relationship?" The women could respond on a nine-point scale from 1 = "I have been very open" to 9 = "I have not been open at all." Tables 6.1 and 6.2 show how varied these women are in how they choose to handle this issue.

As you can see, a large number of women are either very open with their mothers (31.6 percent) or very closed (27.3 percent). The rest are distributed somewhere in between, though more than half regard themselves as being quite open (responses 1, 2, and 3) with their mothers (52.9 percent). Over a third, however, are quite closed (responses 7, 8, and 9: 36.4 percent). The pattern is the same for fathers, though women are not quite as open with their fathers as they are with their mothers. The mean degree of openness for the group as a whole is 4.5 for mothers and 5.2 for fathers.

Many women handle the relationships with their parents amicably and without explicitly discussing lesbianism.

"My mother was always very supportive of anything I did. It was never discussed as a 'relationship' but was taken for granted. My father felt that my partner was like another daughter and enjoyed knowing her.

"My partner's mother didn't approve of our 'lifestyle,' but liked me personally and came to accept the situation with fairly good grace." (Victoria, age 70, 31-year couple)

For some women, entering a committed relationship means dealing with one's parents about lesbianism for the first time. Lauren and Beverly, now a thirteen-year couple, found their getting together inhibited by Lauren's unresolved relationship with her parents. Lauren is now 47, Beverly, 58. Both are Jewish.

Lauren: I had never really come out to my parents. We had a crisis when I was 21 — they found some letters and dragged me off to a psychiatrist — and at the time I led my parents to believe that I was going to try to go straight. We've never talked about

258

it since. Of course they know damn well that that's not what happened.

Beverly: Her mother and father have never really let up: "What clothes do you wear when you go out? What do you talk about when you meet a guy?"

Lauren: Well, they're not so bad any more. But I am an only child, and come from a Jewish background, and it was really devastating to them.

Susan: What in particular about a Jewish background?

Lauren: Jews are very, very family oriented. I mean, if you're not married, you're nothing. You're not an adult unless you're married.

Beverly: A woman, unless she's married and makes babies, does not exist.

Lauren: So, I visited my parents when Beverly and I were just trying to get together. I would have been 34 years old or so. The day I was leaving my mother said, "Well, you want to get married, don't you?" And I said, "No, I don't." She looked absolutely shocked. I said, "I have a very nice life, there is nobody that I care to marry, and I don't see that that should be my goal." She didn't know what to say. But that's all I said. I didn't admit anything else, and she didn't ask.

I was very shaken by the whole thing. When I got off the plane, I was absolutely in tears.

Beverly: She was a terrible mess.

Lauren: Because I realized that there was no

way that I could live with Beverly yet, because of all this unresolved stuff, you see. It was almost a year after that — after a lot of counseling — that we finally did move in together.

Susan: So in effect you got up your nerve to deal with your family so that you could make this relationship work.

Lauren: Well, I needed to do it anyway; this was the catalyst.

Beverly: She established herself as an adult with them. It was hard.

Some relationships with parents continue to be close and satisfying to the daughter, and can develop to include her partner in an intimate way. Not only do we look for support from our parents; increasingly as we and they age, we find ways to support them. Martha also is Jewish.

"I think one of the most touching experiences of our relationship was this year when my father became ill in Los Angeles. I had difficulty taking care of him. Bonnie flew down immediately and helped me move him back to Minneapolis. He lived with us for three months. Bonnie was not only wonderful, caring, and supportive, but took a real role in his recovery (she's a naturopath). It made me feel like we were a real family. And now that he's better, we do things as a family.

"It was an event that brought us closer. I'm blessed to have Bonnie as my partner." (Martha, age 36, 10-year couple)

Several of the couples have spent significant portions of their lives together living with and taking care of their parents, most often mothers.

A nineteen-year couple have been taking care of one woman's mother for ten years. It is not easy. In response to the question about the biggest source of problems, the daughter says, "My mother and the way she is critical and judgmental of our (and especially my partner's) actions." Her partner says, "Her mother, who lives with us and has for ten years and will for the rest of her life." These women are ages 45 and 55.

For Norma, age 67, and Elsie, age 73, it was more satisfying. They took care of Elsie's mother for about ten years.

Norma: Then we moved back to California and bought a place with about twenty acres. She brought her Granny with her.
Susan: That's your Mom, Elsie?
Elsie: Yeah.
Norma: She stayed with us till she got so bad that we had to fly her back to a nursing home in Peoria, because we felt she should be with the family, where they could get to her once in a while. So then Elsie went back home for a couple of years.
Susan: Oh really?
Norma: Because Granny was too bad to leave alone, and Elsie is not the type to leave her mother alone.
Elsie: Well, I was the only one that was free to watch over her.
Norma: That was no sacrifice. You know, if it

261

had been my mother she'd have done the same.

The women in four of the five couples who have done major caretaking of their mothers are at least 65 years old, and five of the ten women are in their 70s. (I did not specifically ask about care-taking of parents. There thus may be more of it being done by lesbian couples than was volunteered in the questionnaires.) This may reflect the commitment of their generation to personal caretaking of parents. Or it may simply reflect the fact that "unmarried" daughters in our society take care of parents, and that as the rest of the lesbians' parents reach the ages where they need care, many of these women too will find themselves in this role. I suspect the generational explanation is the more relevant, but we shall see what responsibilities we take on as our parents age.

Norma and Elsie have a story about Elsie's mother that will help you appreciate what this couple did for her; she also did plenty for them. Years earlier, when Norma and Elsie were getting to know each other, Elsie had just gone through a disturbing breakup with a domineering partner of many years. Elsie's ex-partner sent her home to Peoria, Illinois, to get herself together, and presumably to return to her. Norma stayed behind in Portland, Oregon, where they all lived.

> *Elsie:* I was crying around there in Illinois and Mom — I was living with Mother — I told her a little bit about it all, about my ex and about Norma, and so she said, "I'm

gonna write." She says, "Give me a paper and pencil." So she says, "What's Norma's address there in Oregon?" I told her. She writes, "Dear Norma, Wouldn't you like to stop by and have a cup of coffee?"
Norma: So I did.

Table 6.3 shows you how supportive the lesbians in this study feel their parents are. The question was, "To what extent are your parents supportive of your relationship?" The responses (on the nine-point scale) ranged from 1 = "Extremely supportive" to 9 = "Not at all supportive."

There is such variability in the degree to which lesbians in long-term couples experience support from their parents, that I asked in interviews whether couples felt it made any difference to them whether they were close to their families-of-origin or not. They agreed that being close with families was good if you

TABLE 6.3 HOW SUPPORTED THE WOMEN FEEL BY THEIR PARENTS

Degree of support	From mothers (% of women)	From fathers (% of women)
Women who feel quite a bit of support (Responses 1,2,3)	54.6	44.1
Women who feel only moderate levels of support (Rs 4,5,6)	25.0	32.5
Women who feel little or no support (Rs 7,8,9)	20.4	23.4
Total	100.0	100.0

had it, and difficult if you didn't, but in either case it was not crucial to their couple relationship.

Here's how Ginny and Virginia, a twenty-three-year couple, feel about family support. Ginny's parents are dead, Virginia's mother and a stepfather are still alive.

Ginny: My parents knew about us, but it was never, ever discussed.

Susan: Did it seem like they were supportive?

Ginny: My dad was; my mother was not. But then she wasn't supportive of anything I ever did.

Virginia: I'm sure my brothers and sisters all suspect. My parents know. My family's very supportive of Ginny. They like to have her around.

Susan: Do you think that's significant in staying together, having family support? Or is that just a nice thing to have if you have it?

Ginny: It's a nice thing.

Virginia: It's a nice thing to have.

Ginny: I don't think it's significant.

Virginia: No. If you don't have it, you just stay away from them, stay away from the problem.

I'm reminded of Rena, in the story that preceded this chapter, whose mother had to learn that Rena and Mattie's family could go on without her. If she wanted to be part of it, she had to find it within herself to be accepting and forthcoming. She had to join them.

This, it seems to me, is at least part of the story. If parents and siblings want to share our experience to some degree, either with full knowledge of our lesbianism, or simply with the knowledge that we care for each other, they are welcome — in fact, very welcome. If they cannot bring themselves to accept us to some degree, our lives will go on without them, regretfully perhaps, even with anguish, but fully.

The other part of the story is that we need to give them the chance to be their best selves. If their participation in our lives is at all important to us, we need to invite them in, and to challenge their prejudices and stereotypes. We should not let them abuse us or our partners, we should set boundaries so they must recognize us as the couple we are, and we should expect the best of them. If they then fail us, at least we have tried. And they can always come around tomorrow — or next year — when they've had a chance to think better of it.

Children

Sixty percent of the long-term couples are made up of women, neither of whom has had children. Table 6.4 summarizes the data about the presence of children in long-term couples.

Most couples who do not have children are in agreement about not wanting them.

> "I haven't had a desire for children, and I was lucky to find a partner who also has no need of motherhood. Somehow that 'motherly drive' didn't hit us! However, we feel we could

TABLE 6.4 HOW MANY COUPLES HAVE CHILDREN?

Does this couple have children?	Number of couples	Percent of couples
No children in this couple	65	60.2
Prior children, but not relevant to this couple	12	11.1
Prior children, and they have been/ are relevant to this couple	18	16.7
Children acquired as part of this couple	13	12.0
Total	108	100.0

have done a good job of raising children if it had happened." (Jane, age 52, 31-year couple)

"There is no place for children in our relationship. Given the style of living to which we have become accustomed and the expectations of attention we have for one another, children would be an undesirable invasion." (This woman is a very satisfied kindergarten teacher, age 37, 12-year couple)

But for other couples the issue is more difficult.

"We have discussed raising a child in this relationship. Fran is unable to have biological children and uninterested. My biological clock is ticking. I am still able to but am not sure I want to take on what I perceive to be the responsibility and disruption and conflict adding a child to this relationship would mean.

Until my desire/motivation is a whole lot stronger, Fran and I will not be parenting a child together." (Nancy, age 35, 12-year couple)

Her partner says,

"Interest in children has never occurred for me. Not even my dolls had 'babies.'" (Fran, age 40)

Many lesbians who do not themselves have children find some way to incorporate children into their lives. Often they work with children.

"We have chosen not to have children of our own, but are intentionally involved with children of friends and with a niece. We plan special time to be with these children and to be part of each other's lives." (Kathy, age 48, 13-year couple)

"Both my partner and I are strong advocates for children in our work, she in adoption, me in child clinical psychology. We have shared many cases and have long-term social relationships with some families, e.g., attending special events, taking kids to the country for weekends. We are treated as 'special friends' in some families." (Leigh, age 58, 26-year couple)

In twelve long-term lesbian couples one or both women have had children, but these children have never been directly relevant to this particular couple, e.g., they grew up before the women ever got together, or they stayed with the woman's husband when she divorced, etc.

Thirty-one of the long-term couples, however, have been significantly involved with children in one way or another in the course of their relationship. For eighteen of the couples, one or both women had children in a previous relationship and brought them to this couple for significant amounts of childrearing. Thirteen couples have chosen to have children themselves, through artificial insemination, sex with a male donor, or adoption.

Couples Who Have "Inherited" Children from Prior Relationships

Donna is 35 and the mother of a 16-year-old son. The child resulted from one contact with a man, who was never involved in the son's parenting. Donna and her partner Faye have raised this boy fulltime for twelve years. Donna says:

> "Essentially my partner and I have shared equally in the decision-making, education, and the development of values since our beginning . . . (She discusses some problems) . . . We learned what parenting was all about together. All the various roles were new. Our son took to my partner very quickly, which was helpful to say the least. Our son was also aware from the start about our relationship.
>
> "Knowing my son truly loves, respects, and

268

learns from my partner also enriches my love for her. Knowing that if I die tomorrow, he will be loved, protected, and cared for by my partner provides me great comfort. Knowing that for today I have her to share my decisions regarding my son enriches our personal relationship."

Faye says:

"I have been a stepparent to a son for the past twelve years. I have been very active in parenting — truly equally shared responsibility — and most of the time it's been a joy. He's been a *big* focus of my life since his mom and I met."

Not all lesbians in long-term couples are open about their lesbianism with the children they are raising. It is my impression that this is particularly true when the children come from a prior relationship. Suzanne, age 51, the mother of a boy and a girl, has now been in her relationship for nineteen years.

"The children were 10 and 12 when we went through a very messy divorce. My partner and I raised them from then until they were each eighteen under trying and difficult circumstances, totally non-supported.

"We did not discuss our relationship with them, although my partner was clear from the beginning about being gay. I talked to my daughter openly in her early twenties, have never told my son about my partner's and my relationship. My daughter maintains a warm relationship with us both (although it has been a struggle), my son is distant and surface polite. Maintaining any kind of contact with him is difficult."

There is agreement among these parents that raising children has its costs as well as its pleasures, that some periods are worse than others, and that the unalloyed pleasures may come after the costs. Here Mollie, a 41-year-old co-parent, describes this progression.

"Fourteen to fifteen years ago, when our relationship began and the children were at home (ages 14, 12, and 9), they were a major part of our lives together, often the focus of conflicts, especially in working out different parenting roles and styles. They were also a delight and a bonus for us; we had other people to care about and relate to.

"Now that the children are adults, my relationship with them is, of course, more equal in terms of friendship. I value my relationship with them and they seem to enrich and deepen the relationship I have with their mother.

"As adults, they are no longer the topic of our fights/arguments/disagreements, though often they are a part of our awareness and discussions."

Some lesbian parents feel that children contribute

to the longevity of their relationship. (Although their presence is clearly not crucial, since most of the long-term lesbian relationships do not involve children.)

"My partner has two children, one girl, one boy. I have lived with her since they were one and four; they are now 15 and 18. I have not played much of a parenting role, which is probably good, since my parenting skills aren't that good. I think the presence of children has contributed to the longevity of our relationship. They've kept us from focusing exclusively on each other." (Judy, age 36, 15-year couple)

Some of the couples who have raised children from prior relationships by this time have grandchildren.

"My lover and I have always lived with my children. For a brief period they were all gone, but circumstances have forced us to live with my one daughter and her child. Children and family are very important to me because of my Native culture and beliefs. I have two grandsons, and they are ever more important to my lover and myself." (Janet, age 48, 13-year couple)

Couples Who've Chosen To Have Children

One might think that these couples who have chosen to have children would find the impact of children more tolerable than those couples who found themselves faced with children as the faits accomplis of one of the women. I don't know if that's true, but I do know that some couples who have chosen to have children find childbearing very difficult and sometimes divisive.

Maureen and Pat, now in their mid-30s, are a fourteen-year couple with two boys, ages 7 and 2. Each woman is the birth mother of one boy, both of whom were conceived through artificial insemination. Pat talks about the impact of having children:

"Children have changed our relationship tremendously! Prior to kids we had a solid, nurturing, and in some ways, trouble-free relationship. As we had kids, our relationship slowly shifted to an emotionally distant, stressful, and sometimes difficult one.

"I believe when you have kids, the 'slices of the pie' get smaller and smaller. Kids take a huge chunk, then what's left you have to divide up between work, friends, and the relationship. In our case, the relationship came last, which clearly took its toll. We are now in the process of getting ourselves back in balance."

Even with all these difficulties, Pat feels the children have helped keep the relationship together.

"Children have definitely kept us together. Also, we've made an 'investment' in the relationship; we've put a lot into this relationship, too much to just throw it away."

Perhaps the truth is that children can be both divisive — their presence causes enough trouble to make you think about breaking up — and connecting — you find yourself unwilling to break up and lose them and all you've put into this larger family structure.

This matter of balancing the demands of children with the desire to keep one's couple relationship primary is critical. Joy and Linda are a ten-year couple with a one-year-old adopted son.

> *Linda:* The baby has added a new dimension. It is something we both wanted, 100 percent. It is hard at times but, like investments, momentary discomfort that reaps boundless rewards if enough thought, planning, and education is put into it. I think we both enjoy the challenges parenthood provides.
>
> I also would like to note that our primary relationship remains paramount, in spite of the deep love we have for Nick.

Some lesbian couples who choose to have children adopt a lifestyle oriented much more toward family than toward lesbian community. Kate and Marilyn have been together nineteen years. Each of them has given birth to a child: Kate's son is now 12, Marilyn's daughter is 5.

They talk about a group of former lesbian friends who, it seemed to them, drank too much and exchanged partners a lot. Kate,

"I never knew from one day to the next who was with who. We just decided that wasn't for us."

They moved away from this group, further south, to the suburbs of Boston.

Susan: You didn't try to reproduce that kind of lesbian friendship network here?
Kate: No, we tried to get away from that. We were already discussing having children. The lesbians we are close to now are people that have been together for a long time. Otherwise we've just gone more with family-type people.
Marilyn: We had a family nearby that we got close to . . .
Kate: They had different sexual preferences, but very similar values.
Susan: Like what?
Kate: Like being interested in family. Their ideas of a good time would be going to a movie or just getting together rather than going to a bar. We'd get together once a week and do a craft, some kind of artistic thing.

Of course lesbian couples with children are not just like heterosexual families. We have our own problems and our own triumphs.

274

Marilyn: Our being lesbians has become more of an issue now that Steve's gotten older, because at 12 he's aware.

Susan: What did you do with your kids about that?

Kate: We're real open, we're real openly affectionate.

Marilyn: Real open, but open without labels.

Kate: Open without labels. And that was a mistake. We should have given him more labels.

Marilyn: He's always known, on some level. But at school one day someone asked him, and he said "Heavens, no." Then he came home and asked Kate, "Mom, you're not a lesbian, are you?"

Kate: I said, "Well, yes, I am."

Marilyn: It ruined him.

Kate: He had a real hard time. He was real sad. I think it was all the implications he had to deal with. He liked his mom, and here was all that crap coming from school. . . .

We even took him to a counselor, a man. It amounted to two sessions, though they were very helpful to Stevie. He just needed to be told. The counselor said to him, "Look, there are a lot of different people in the world. Your mother's a nice woman and so's the woman she lives with. So don't let the rest get in your way."

Marilyn: Basically he told Steve, "Really, it's none of your business. What your mother does in her bed is really none of your business."

Kate: "And what you do in yours is none of her business." And that seemed to be all it took.

At the end the counselor said to me, "He's the most well-adjusted child I have ever dealt with. Go home and count your blessings."

Kate and Marilyn agree, however, that even with all its rewards and glories, having children is hard.

Marilyn: A lot of lesbian couples have asked us about having kids. They want to know how you know if you should. We usually end up recommending to most of them not to. There's nothing more stressful than the first six months after the child arrives. I mean, your life will change more in that first six months than it ever has or maybe will again.

Kate: And if your relationship isn't really strong to begin with, you might as well kiss it good-bye. Because there isn't anything that's going to wedge between the two of you more than children. I mean, even physically. They plant themselves right in the middle. You go to hug your partner, and they. . . .

Marilyn: We used to call Steve "Wedgie."

I think that what these mothers are trying to tell us is that raising children can be a wonderful experience, but we should know that it is an experience that completely changes your couple relationship for the twenty or so years these children are dependent upon you. Pat: "Kids have enriched our lives/relationship, but not without consequence."

Even with all the warnings and sober evaluation, though, it seems that the desire of some of us to be intimately involved with children is unquenchable. Lucky for those children.

> *Kate:* You can set up people's expectations so your children can have the best. I've always presented my children as though I think they are very smart, they are very personable, they are wonderful, and you are lucky to know them.
>
> *Marilyn:* I went into my son's teacher and said, "I want you to meet Stevie Robertson, your gifted child for the year."

And lucky for us.

> "As I fill out this questionnaire we are waiting for the baby we are adopting to be born. (I mean literally waiting; the birth mother is in labor.). . . .
>
> "I can't believe I'm actually filling this in tonight. I feel so distracted because of the baby! I'm excited, scared, terrified, happy, etc. about adding to our family.
>
> "Having a child in my life is very important to me, and my partner has changed her mind from negative to positive. We both intend to be active parents, and I believe we

will be a great team." (Sara, age 38, 17-year couple)

Friends

Friends are important to the women in these long-term lesbian couples. Most of them are open — in the sense of acknowledging being lesbians — with their lesbian friends, more open, as you might expect, than they are with anyone else. Table 6.5 shows how open the women in long-term couples feel they are with heterosexual friends and co-workers. Table 6.6 shows, by contrast, how open they are with gay male friends, and lesbian friends.

Lesbians in long-term couples are quite open with both co-workers and heterosexual friends. Often this openness means allowing others to perceive you as a couple, but not going so far as to use the "L" word.

"I'm sure most of our friends are aware of our relationship, and we're regarded as a

TABLE 6.5 HOW OPEN THE WOMEN ARE WITH HETEROSEXUAL FRIENDS AND CO-WORKERS

Degree of openness	Heterosexual friends (% of women)	Co-workers (% of women)
Very open (Responses 1,2,3)	49.1	39.8
Moderately open (Rs 4,5,6)	20.3	20.9
Not very open (Rs 7,8,9)	30.6	39.3
Totals	100.0	100.0

TABLE 6.6 HOW OPEN THE WOMEN ARE WITH GAY MALE AND LESBIAN FRIENDS

Degree of openness	Gay male friends (% of women)	Lesbian friends (% of women)
Very open (Responses 1,2,3)	88.5	96.2
Moderately open (Rs 4,5,6)	5.2	1.4
Not very open (Rs 7,8,9)	6.3	2.4
Totals	100.0	100.0

'couple,' often being the only same-sex couple at dinners or other parties, but the relationship isn't verbalized, and we're just accepted. Just as I wouldn't quiz friends on their personal marital situations, I wouldn't be inclined to discuss mine with others." (Victoria, age 70, 31-year couple)

With gay male friends and other lesbians, however, the vast majority of women in long-term relationships feel they can be very open. Of the 213 women who answered the question, 185 feel they have been "very open" (response = 1) with lesbian friends.

Lesbians say their friends are important supports for their long-term relationships. In response to the question about what forms the heart of a successful relationship, Eudora, a 60-year-old woman in a twenty-year couple includes, "A good group of friends with the same ideals and morals. No fooling around!"

The importance of friends is often articulated when the women give advice for other women who want to stay together:

"Develop a circle of friends with whom you can be totally honest." (Jeanine, age 41, 10-year couple)

"Have other friends who are couples, who support your committed relationship." (Emily, age 39, 11-year couple)

"Find other lesbians who want, have, and believe in long-term relationships." (Ellen, age 37, 13-year couple)

There's an underlying theme here. These women are not talking about just any friends; they specifically advocate the importance of friends who value being in couples.

Some couples believe they might have broken up had it not been for the intervention and support of friends. Laura and Robin have been together twelve years.

Laura: During the seventh year of the relationship we almost broke up. What made the difference was the help of some friends who gave us a different perspective on the relationship and the difficulties we were experiencing.

Robin: Our friends came and said, "You can't do this to us."

Laura: "You can't do it. If you think you really want to break up, you have to sit down and talk to us."

Robin: They made us make contracts with each other. And we did.

Susan: How loving.

Robin: Yes. We were really fortunate.

Robin and Laura were able to return this gift because a year or so later their friends, Melissa and Amy, almost broke up themselves. Robin and Laura helped see them through this difficult time. Melissa in her questionnaire describes the episode.

"We almost broke up the time my partner was very depressed for a long time and counseling didn't seem to help . . . We had lots of family and friend support to hang in there." (age 37, 12-year couple)

Another couple feels that friends are among the three most significant factors that explain why they have stayed together.

"Factor 3. We have an amazing group of friends and family who support our relationship." (Nell, age 36, 11-year couple)

Her partner acknowledges that Nell and she have become role models, that their long partnership contributes something to the community.

"Last November we had a ten-year anniversary party with our lesbian friends and my sisters. It was a fine time. The community itself was excited for us, and specific individuals were hopeful that they too could make commitments because they had now really seen a 'long' relationship." (Phyllis, age 37)

Not all the long-term couples feel the community supports their relationship. Although all find friends important, some believe the lesbian community is hostile to the idea of long, committed relationships:

"Lack of community support, and this includes the lesbian community. I think relationships are not taken seriously, and people are often unwilling/unable to work at staying together. The 'grass always looks greener,' and people continue to be lonely." (Jennie, age 37, 18-year couple)

A couple who have just moved to a large city with a big lesbian population say,

"We first got together when we were living in a small town of 20,000. Being coupled seems more of the norm in a small town atmosphere than in Seattle. There was more social support for being a couple there, but it was rough to break up." (Sandra, age 38, 12-year couple)

A seventeen-year couple believes that the most significant factor in their having stayed together is, "being isolated from the lesbian community."

The women in long-term couples are very grateful for their close friends. They have fun with them.

Here Gertie, a 65-year-old woman in a 39-year couple, describes the enterprise she, her partner, and another couple have undertaken.

"We bought five acres of raw land up in Montana and proceeded to have a grand time! . . . The four of us shared in the cost of everything. We opened a bank account just for the 'Ranch' expenses, and each couple had a checkbook. There was a lot of trust, and we shared everything. The property is in joint tenancy with the last one alive being left with everything. One partner has passed away, but the remaining three are carrying on."

Harriet reminds us — if we need reminding — of one of the points of friendship for lesbians:

"Close lesbian friends, many of whom had very long, stable relationships (up to fifty years) have been very important to me. In part, it has created a sense of family who share my lifestyle. I can be myself with them and don't have to hide my love for my partner." (age 42, 17-year couple)

The Larger Society

It is easy to forget, when talking with long-term couples, that we lesbians live in a society that disapproves of and discriminates against us. The couples are, for the most part, so integrated into their neighborhoods and professions, so productive and so respectable, that it is shocking to think they have all had to deal — to a greater or lesser extent — with opposition because of their lesbianism. But the fact is, they have; the undertone of loss and grief is there.

"Being in the closet and dealing with societal discrimination has been a persistent pressure and source of frustration. We have chosen a middle path. We are out to friends and some siblings, we don't announce to others but we don't completely hide. We both feel like coming out at work would be a risk, but we resent having to lead a split life.

"At one point we considered having a child, but decided it would exacerbate the problem." (Kim, age 37, 18-year couple)

There is a moderate perception of actual discrimination among these lesbians. Fifty-four percent say they have experienced no discrimination in their jobs. But this leaves 46 percent who have experienced some form of job discrimination because they are lesbians. Nearly 15 percent believe they have lost jobs sometime during their careers because of their lesbianism.

I asked the question, "How much do you care whether heterosexuals know you are a lesbian?" Table 6.7 gives the responses.

The most refreshing answer to this question was the lesbian who said, "I would be upset if *anyone* thought I might be heterosexual." (Barbara, age 54, 17-year couple)

But more typically this question was an opportunity for some of the women to tell us how

TABLE 6.7 HOW MUCH DO THE WOMEN CARE WHO KNOWS THEY ARE LESBIAN?

Response	Number of women	Percent of women
I do not care who knows I am a lesbian	46	22.0
There are a few heterosexuals I do not want to know I am a lesbian	78	37.3
There are a large number of heterosexuals I do not want to know I am a lesbian	76	36.4
I do not want any heterosexuals to know I am a lesbian	9	4.3
Totals	209*	100.0

*Number of women responding to this question.

they handle being open or closed in various settings. Work is crucial because work is so important to us, and we are so vulnerable there (thus, I believe, the large number of lesbians who've chosen self-employment).

"There are a large number of heterosexuals I do not want to know I am a lesbian because I work with children, and too many people do not have an appropriate understanding." (Sue, age 39, 11-year couple)

"I personally don't care (who knows) but it would undercut my credibility as an expert witness in court cases about child custody, so I wouldn't come out professionally." (Anne, age 58, 26-year couple)

285

We are much safer in our homes. But still 8.4 percent of these women have experienced discrimination in housing, e.g., with landlords or mortgage companies. Small wonder 83 percent of the women own their own homes, effectively protecting themselves from such discrimination.

A tone of extreme care underlies many of the responses.

> "I have always endeavored — and with quite a degree of success — to make people comfortable with me as a person and not in the context of my lifestyle. What conclusions they draw from knowing me doesn't seem to change how they interact with me." (Victoria, age 70, 31-year couple)

This is probably how many of us handle the problem of being out to straight co-workers and other heterosexuals.

> "Most know, but not by talking about it. We are always included as a couple at functions in any of their homes." (Winona, age 55, 19-year couple)

This sounds like an okay arrangement; we're all so accustomed to it. As long as we don't mention anything explicitly, the "outside world" is willing to tolerate us, in fact to like and value us. We know, though, that they have little conscious awareness, really, of who we are. And if they did know, we fear their friendship and support would evaporate. We maintain a constant vigilance, no less damaging just because it has become second nature.

Some women are so terrified by the thought of exposure — and whatever that might bring — that they can remember specifically the times they have revealed themselves to someone other than other gay people.

"I do not want any heterosexuals to know I am a lesbian, except the three I've told in my life (one in 1976, one in 1979, one in 1986)." (Sarah, age 39, 13-year couple)

Sarah expresses the anguish we all feel wherever it is in our lives we feel we have to hide.

"I wish I didn't have to be in the closet. I wish my parents and all others close to me could know what a wonderful loving relationship I have. I hate hiding something I wish the whole world could know."

It is a reality of living as lesbians that we are always aware at some level of the stigma of our status as . . . what should we call ourselves? . . . our status as "outlaw lovers." We all live with care and an ear alert for the whisperings of danger. Little surprise we value so much whoever we have found we can count on: certainly, our friends and — if we are lucky, and have done some hard work — to some degree, our families.

STORY 7:

DEBORAH (age 39) & KATHY (age 48): 13 years together

Deborah and Kathy are a thirteen-year couple living in Chicago. Lately they are feeling that their relationship has gotten easier. But first we talked about earlier difficulties.

Deborah: It has certainly felt easy recently. There have been several rough periods in our history, and a couple of rotten times.
Kathy: A couple? I only remember one.
Deborah: One other time that was rocky.

Kathy: We've had some things we've had to deal with, but none that have really come between us or that we had to overcome or work out or figure out or concede, except this one thing.

Deborah: It's felt pretty easy these last few years.

Susan: How did you get past the one thing?

Kathy: We went to therapy.

Susan: What does that do for you that you couldn't do for yourselves? Or that you wouldn't do for yourselves?

Kathy: It just puts things in perspective.

Deborah: It's somebody on the outside saying, "Take a look at this. What are you really doing here?"

Kathy: Our therapist said to us, "It's big — the issue is big — but is it so important that you gotta split up over it?"

The situation was that I made a decision to convert to Judaism. It was kind of a blow.

Deborah: I hated it. I just hated it. She couldn't have picked a worse thing to do.

Kathy was raised in a devout Methodist family, spent considerable time in the Episcopal Church, and had been thinking for awhile about the spiritual meaning Judaism might have for her. Deborah was raised Jewish and grew up in a Jewish community, though her family was never traditionally religious. She had never thought about Judaism as a particular focus of her life, not until just before Kathy got her idea of converting five years ago.

Susan: What was it about Kathy's idea that you hated so much?

Deborah: It was a time that I was coming to terms with my own Jewish identity and all the internalized hatred and shame I had about it. I was just starting to open up and feel real good about it, and here comes Kathy wanting to convert. I thought, "This is *my* thing to do now. This is mine! Do something else."

Susan: That makes a lot of sense.

Deborah: So it really was a lot about timing.

Susan: Kathy, why did you pick that time?

Kathy: It was something I had thought about for a long time, and this just felt like the time.

Unlike other issues this couple had dealt with in the past, this one was not negotiable.

Kathy: Naive me, I assumed she'd be supportive, and it would be okay . . . Wrong. But I knew that's what I was going to do, and I wasn't not going to do it because she couldn't handle it.

Deborah: That was the first time that had happened.

Kathy: That was the first thing that had ever come up that I didn't feel I could negotiate, that was that important.

Susan: It was just, I'm gonna do this, and that's all there is to it?

Kathy: Yeah, and I don't remember that ever happening with either of us.

Deborah: That was a good challenge to our relationship.

Susan: Were you considering breaking up about this?

Deborah: I think we were. We hadn't exactly talked that far. . . .

Kathy: We were just really at each other all the time, and very very unhappy. We'd set it aside and not talk about it, but it was still there.

Deborah: It never got better. Then Kathy went to see this lesbian rabbi, and the rabbi said I should come see her. First I said, "Tell the rabbi to shove it." Then I went to see her.

She helped. She said, "I see couples all the time who divorce over this. But they have already had lots of other problems about other things. Your relationship is not like that." She was very confronting and very positive. She said, "What are you doing here, risking such a good relationship over this issue?"

Deborah talked about what all this meant for her own identity as a Jew, her own sense of Jewishness.

Deborah: One of the things that was hard was that Kathy was going to learn all this stuff I didn't know about Judaism; she was going to be the good Jew.

The rabbi said, "Easy for you to say, you don't have to do anything to be Jewish; Kathy does." She challenged me to

292

think outside what I was experiencing. I was so into what this meant for me that I couldn't see what Kathy might be feeling at all. The rabbi also talked to me about the fact that not only did I not have to do anything to be a Jew, but she said that I, I was a good Jew.

Kathy and Deborah have class differences to deal with as well. Kathy's background is poor, rural Midwestern. Deborah's is Eastern suburban upper middle class.

Kathy: There's always been a thing for me about money and about saving and about paying my own way. Education was really important, and I went to college, but if you're working class, you never feel like you belong there.

Deborah: I grew up in an upper middle class suburb of Philadelphia. I've always had this sense of belonging, of security and optimism about things working out, about money being there when I need it.

For a long time in their relationship, Kathy and Deborah would find themselves irritated with each other about certain things, about how to have vacations, and how much to worry about money. Once they realized these differences originated with their class backgrounds, they read books about class issues and attended a consciousness-raising group. Eventually, instead of fighting or feeling irritated with each other, they'd say, "Oh, that's just class stuff."

Until recently they have had similar incomes and have shared everything equally, each feeling she should pay her own way. Now, however, Kathy is in school, earning half what Deborah does. Deborah is paying a much larger share of the expenses.

Susan: Does that feel okay, for both of you?
Deborah: To me it does, it feels like a loosening of something.
Kathy: I think one thing I did about it was that I just stopped worrying about money like I have my whole life. I just started to trust my own process, my own direction, instead of getting all hung up and trying to figure everything out way ahead of time. It's a big change for me.

I asked Kathy and Deborah about their sexual lives together.

Susan: How important is sex to you?
Kathy: It's important.
Deborah: Yep, it's important. Not the most important thing, but it's up there. We pay attention to it.
Susan: What do you do to pay attention to it?
Kathy: Well, you know, you can get real comfortable, in your daily activities, and you can forget to take time for yourselves, whether it's for sex or just to take a walk.

There are periods of time when we're not being sexual, but we try to acknowledge

294

that we're not being sexual right now, that it is important, and that we're committed to it.

Susan: Why do you think sex is important enough to pay special attention to it?

Deborah: For me it's a real important connection we have. We all talk a lot about it being hard for lesbians to stay sexual cause it's so comfortable being friends. But it's not so comfortable for me. I notice and feel there's a certain tension, something missing, something out of whack when we're not sexual. I start getting kind of irritable . . . I notice, and it's not right.

For me, sex is a real affirmation of our intimacy.

Kathy: Of who we are and why we're together. I mean, we're not roommates! You know, there's more to being together than splitting a house payment. It has to do with the depth of the connection we have. And there's a part of that connection that is only touched when we're sexual. It's not a part of our relationship that I want to give up.

I know that I change when we don't make time for being sexual; I know I just close down some. There's a part of me that closes off. So when we're not being sexual on a day-to-day basis, there's a part of me that's not giving in other ways either.

It's so important to keep that sense of giving flowing.

Deborah: I also notice that when we are

sexual, afterwards everything feels different.
I mean, I feel different . . . something flows
better.

Kathy: I feel that the quality of our sexual
relationship has really improved. It has
always been good, right from the beginning,
but it has just gotten better.

Susan: What does that mean, quality?

Kathy: It's just more and more satisfying. It's
just incredible. When we're sexual, it's just
incredible.

Deborah: Part of it for me is that I'm not
worrying about it. I trust that it's going to
happen, that we're keeping track enough so
I don't need to worry, "God, it's been three
weeks, I hope this is good."

Kathy: There aren't a lot of shoulds.

Susan: As you talk about these different issues
— religion, and money, and sex — it seems
that one of the things that's characterized
your relationship is one or the other of you
relaxing around what were once issues.

Deborah: (chuckles) That's true.

Kathy: Yeah.

Susan: Which makes me think back to the
beginning of our talk, when you said the
relationship has felt real easy lately. How
do you make something feel easy?

Deborah: I feel like we don't carry a lot of
baggage around with us.

Kathy: We've really learned how to just leave
things . . . how to just leave things behind.

Toward the end of the interview we talked about fighting styles.

Susan: Do you fight? How do you fight?

Kathy: We don't.

Deborah: We don't fight a lot. We get picky sometimes. You know from the earlier discussion why we both can get irritable. . . . (Laughter)

We used to have fights that would start at parties. We'd fight all the way home, and go to bed, turn over, backs to each other, wake up the next morning feeling rotten. The next day we'd come together and say, okay, let's have a truce.

Susan: Would you try to talk about whatever it was before you went to sleep, or would you just agree to drop it?

Kathy: Sometimes we'd try to talk about it, and sometimes just in talking about it, it would get worse. You know, you're in the middle of it, you're tired and crabby . . . you don't negotiate very well when you're defending your position.

Deborah: For us it would work better to go to sleep than to try to stay up all night arguing until we felt better, cause we never did.

Kathy: It always felt better in the morning cause you're more rested.

Deborah: It's a very different style that's developed in the last year or two; we don't seem to need to talk things through until they're resolved. We stopped needing to do that.

Kathy: It doesn't mean things don't get solved, or that they get ignored, but we find that if we don't try to resolve it right then, but wait till we feel better, there's nothing to solve . . . it's solved itself. Or if there is something to be solved, we're better able to see what we need to do, and then we can do it, together.

Deborah: That change isn't something that just sprang up. We've talked about how to do it, and we've tried it.

Kathy: And it's worked really well.

Susan: You mean just dropping stuff, for a while?

Deborah: Some of it just drops out of existence. And some of it, like Kathy said, is just easier later, when you don't feel so riled up.

Kathy: It's like trying to drive through a snow storm when you can't see the road. You can keep driving and risk an accident, or you can stop, wait for the snow to stop, and then drive on and get where you need to go safely.

Of course, the very important issues in our lives can take a long time to be laid to rest. Some of them never are. I asked Kathy and Deborah about disillusionments with each other, things they hoped were going to change about the other person that never did, things they'd perhaps given up on.

Deborah: The thing that occurs to me was when I found out about Kathy being really religious, wanting to be really religious.

Susan: In the sense of organized religion, you mean.

Kathy: I'd really like Deborah to want to be a member of the synagogue; she does go once in a while. She goes more than she ever did, so I'm happy about that. I wanted to have a kosher kitchen too. She threatened to leave the kitchen entirely up to me.

Deborah: I would never have imagined myself being with someone who had religion as a priority. And I didn't know about her religious interest when I met her. The period from the time I met Kathy until her conversion was an aberration in her life. She was being spiritual — something I'm comfortable with — but not religious. Turns out this was very atypical. All the rest of her life, she'd been very religious.

Susan: So how are you dealing with this new truth about her?

Deborah: I accept it. For me, it's a difference. I have my own group, my women's spirituality group, that feels like my primary spiritual expression . . .

Kathy: And I'm not as active, I don't go to synagogue as often as I did before. And Deborah comes with me sometimes.

Susan: So there's a little bit of . . .

Deborah: A little bit of compromise.

Susan: How is it different to be Jewish lesbians than to be just lesbians?

Deborah: That's a whole 'nother three-hour discussion! (Laughter)

Chapter 7
Change and Conclusions

We sometimes make the mistake of thinking long-term relationships are endlessly boring, endlessly the same. Nothing could be further from the truth. Look at the terrors involved: fears of being seen for who we are, of not being good enough to be loved, of being swallowed up, of losing our freedom, of becoming too dependent, of loving too much, of loving not enough, and — in the special case of same-sex

301

relationships — of doing something other people will think is very wrong.

We must let someone else become profoundly important to us. And we must let ourselves become profoundly important to them.

Then, when things get unhappy — and they will — we have to stay there, we have to stick it out, to find a way around or through it. We have to talk and listen, to negotiate and compromise, to give up being right and learn sometimes to do it her way. And then we have to forgive and let wounds heal and be happy again.

Throughout this book the women in long-term couples have guided us along this perilous path. I've shared with you their stories and observations, their mistakes and triumphs, their warnings, and their advice. Much of the story has been told. When there have been conclusions to draw, they've appeared in the chapter on a particular topic. Rather than repeat those conclusions, I'd like to devote this last chapter to some new ideas and some final thoughts.

Everything Changes

By definition, a long-term relationship has to meet the challenge of time. Here's advice from Louise, age 39, from the vantage point of twenty-one years in the same couple: "Be flexible and accepting of the fact that everything changes to some degree over time."

"Over time," those two little words that mean your whole world changes, repeatedly. Over time, some or all of the following can and probably will happen:

— the intense sexuality of the early years declines;

— it becomes necessary to "work" on the relationship;

— traumatic events take place: interests in other women, affairs, the deaths of parents, ill health, moving, changing jobs, retirement;

— unpleasant truths about your partner emerge: she watches football, she's religious;

— one or both of you change in unexpected ways: you want more "space," more separateness; she wants a child.

How do couples cope with all this change? For one thing, they recognize that, while time provides the challenges, time also provides some of the remedy. Time is on their side; they have perspective.

Bad Times Get Better

Polly is a 41-year-old woman who began her twenty-five year relationship when she was 16 years old.

"When you are not enjoying each other, believe that the 'not fun' times are only temporary."

Another woman gives the same advice,

"Expect hard times and know that they

will be as impermanent as the wildly good times (although we have had more than our share of laughs.)" (Debra, age 39, 15-year couple)

One advantage of a long-term relationship is that you have time to realize the truth of this advice: that, in fact, while good times deteriorate into bad times, the bad times also run their course and cycle into good times again. This is how an eighteen-year couple expresses this sense of perspective:

Beryl: We have a sense that life goes on, and we will get through it, and although this is hard right now, it'll pass. It's not the end of the world.

Mary Pat: There's tons of things we've talked about tonight that many, many people I know personally have broken up over. And I know people who have broken up about even smaller things. I think sometimes people don't — this sounds silly, but I think it's true — people don't hang in long enough to know that you can live past it, you can grow past it, it doesn't have to be this big gaping wound, it can heal. People aren't patient enough.

We talked about how hard it is to recognize your part in some problem, to stop blaming your partner and this particular relationship.

Beryl: You have to have time to see that.

Mary Pat: And you have to be willing to see that.

Susan: If you keep changing people, then you can always think it's the other person that is the problem.

Mary Pat: I think a lot of people think the grass is greener. I don't think that. Sure, I could be with someone else, but if it wasn't the problems Beryl and I have, if it wasn't money, if it wasn't employment, if it wasn't sex, it would be something else. There's no such thing as a relationship without conflict, it just ain't gonna happen. You have to have some kind of acceptance of that . . .

Another person isn't the answer. There ain't nothin' out there that's perfect.

Mary Pat is warning us against allowing our instinct for fleeing in the face of pain to carry the day. Being human, we often try to escape hard times in a relationship by escaping the relationship. We become attracted to someone else. Lynne suggests we think of this, not as an attraction, but as a distraction.

"Relationships are very hard work. They don't just happen, and none of them are frictionless or perfect.

"If you don't have fights and problems to work through, then something is wrong. Everyone has to learn to live together, and because of how most of us are raised, it doesn't come naturally; it's not easy. You have to make up/create/discover/learn how to do it.

"Don't give up and run away or get distracted by someone new when things get hard. It's worth it, not only for the relationship, but for your own growth as well, to work through it. If you don't, it will just come up again with someone else." (age 33, 11-year couple)

The passage of time gives you the chance to see that things get better, and worse again, and better again. It also allows you to discover that some problems actually dissipate with time: children who may have caused tension grow up and move into their own lives; the difference in age between you that seemed so significant at first becomes inconsequential in the middle years (It may become significant again as you near the end of your lives); you discover that the sacrifices you each make for the other even out over time — you don't need to "keep track" anymore. Time, just left to itself, can solve some problems with great effectiveness.

Time Heals

Time can also give you a chance to heal. It is inevitable that people who live together intimately for years will hurt each other. Long-term partners must find a way to allow themselves and their partner to heal, to let go of old hurts, to forgive. Carrying around resentments over the short haul is

306

burdensome; over the long haul, it's crippling. I asked the women, "Have the things that have kept you together changed over the years?" Some of them took this opportunity to talk about healing and the increasing ease of their relationship.

"Yes! I never think about breaking up any more. I hardly ever analyze our relationship like I used to. I'm much more easygoing. Both of us are much more peaceful now. Your words 'kept us together' feels like an odd phrase now, as if there is some kind of ongoing force that works against our being together; I haven't felt that in years." (Deborah, age 39, 13-year couple)

"Yes. The love has grown. The hardships we have gone through have made me realize our communication wasn't as good as it could have been. Fear stopped me from being as honest and communicative as I could have been.

"We both did a lot of work on our relationship, and have gotten the trust back, and are more willing than ever to communicate honestly and work on keeping our relationship healthy. I don't have to be right all the time. I can say 'I'm sorry.' I can cop to my part." (Brenda, age 34, 12-year couple)

Forgiveness is a major theme when I ask, "What do you think forms the heart of a successful relationship?"

Willingness to forgive or admit error." (Janet, age 35, 12-year couple)

"Shared, mutual love evolving from . . . recuperating from and forgetting fights and misunderstandings." (Cynthia, age 66, 29-year couple)

"You have to love each other enough to 'find your way back' to each other after arguments or disagreements." (Wendy, age 39, 15-year couple)

Although complete forgiveness, 100 percent letting go of resentments, is the ideal, I suspect one of the bittersweet truths of long-term couples is that all the pain cannot be left behind. Time softens memory, smooths the rough edges of wounds, but each of us somewhere in our core probably remembers forever an echo of how much particular pains hurt. These women have been together eighteen years.

Frances: It's past. Things can be repaired. They may never be brand new again, but then that's life, you know.
Ellen: I think a relationship is richer in many ways. It's damaged, but as a whole, it's richer.
Susan: It's different, not as virginal, not as innocent.

We remember pain, and forgive despite the memory. Perhaps that is the truth of it.

Time Gives Us Memories of the Past, Visions of the Future

Time forces us to remember the pain, but it also allows us to remember the pleasures. Over time we are amassing a treasure of shared experiences; we are building a past with our partner, one we will never have to let go of. Here I'm talking with Kate, a partner in a nineteen-year couple.

> *Susan:* Tell me some more about how you feel you didn't really know each other for years.
> *Kate:* I just think it takes a long time. You don't just walk up to someone and really be intimate and bare your deepest, darkest secrets and feelings; that's a process that develops over the years.
>
> If you break up fast, you never really get to know that person intimately. That takes years and years and years; it probably took us ten years to really know each other.

Long-term couples accumulate memories together; they construct a past for their relationship.

> "There's a real bonus in having a history of experiences together. More time means more knowing and understanding. I like having all the shared memories." (Betsy, age 39, 21-year couple)

And they develop a vision of the future.

"Day in, day out, my relationship with Lori is a basic of my life. I really matter to another person and that person is important to me beyond anyone else. There is both history and a future together." (Eleanor, age 52, 19-year couple)

"I'm really not sure of all the reasons Nan and I are still together and will be for a long, long time. I do know that the thought of growing old with her excites me. I can picture us retired and touring the country." (Adele, age 36, 11-year couple)

"In the future I'm excited to see where I go and where we go." (Jill, age 38, 10-year couple)

If you're committed to a long-term relationship, you get to stay around to see what happens next. Of course, it may be a relief to know that not *everything* that happens next will be a surprise. Kate is talking about arguments she and her partner have.

"So those are little things you have to work out. I'm real used to the things about Marilyn that drive me crazy. And likewise, Marilyn is used to me. If I were with somebody else, I would irritate the shit out of them. I would have to go through all that adjusting all over again. I'm just not up to that. I'm too old. I don't want to be doin' that. I want to be comfortable in my old age,

lover died twenty years ago. Now Alice feels she needs to find Laurie another partner for after she herself is gone.

> *Alice:* Gloria, Laurie's former partner, told me at the beginning she was looking for someone to take her place as Laurie's partner upon her death. Now I find myself in the same position as Gloria was. But Laurie is extremely shy and is not one to make any kind of overture to anyone. So far I have been unsuccessful in finding someone for her.

Though the long-term couples, especially the older women, are aware that death will intervene, I do not get the impression they let the prospect interfere with their day-to-day lives. Elsie and Norma brought up Elsie's mother as someone to emulate.

> *Elsie:* When my mom was in her 80s, 85 about, she was still plantin' trees, and never thought about . . .
> *Norma:* . . . not seeing the tree grow.
> *Elsie:* Her mind was always . . .
> *Norma:* . . . on the future.

Put the Relationship First

Despite themselves — most were very reluctant to presume to give advice — the women in my study have offered a lot of suggestions about how to build a

313

long-term relationship. I think they would agree that among the most important is the admonition to put your relationship first.

"Put your relationship first. Make it the most important thing in your life and attend to it constantly and as the top priority." (Brenda, age 50, 11-year couple)

Judith, a woman in a thirteen-year couple, gives five pieces of advice that summarize what many would say.

"Put your relationship first.
Believe it will last.
Spend time together.
Talk.
Be friends as well as lovers."

Another woman, in a fourteen-year couple, is describing what forms the heart of a successful relationship,

". . . a strong belief that the relationship be placed first, and a willingness to arrange other aspects of life around it, instead of fitting the relationship around other things." (Joyce, age 31)

A thirteen-year couple has operationalized their commitment to putting the relationship first.

"Make your relationship more important than other friends, interests, jobs, etc. Plan special times for *just* the two of you, at least once a week. 'Our night' is real important to us. It includes only each other, no TV, no reading magazines, etc., and usually most begin by 6 p.m." (Lisa, age 39)

A fourth woman, in an eleven-year couple, relates our commitment to a long-term relationship to our capacity for self love.

"I think a lot of the grief we give each other over relationships is an expression of our own internalized self-hate, not really thinking we are worth the care and consideration and time and effort to take care of ourselves and each other. It is a healthy and self-loving, self-respecting thing to make an important relationship a high or the highest priority in your life, and then to live your life based on that decision or realization." (Mary Jo, age 33)

Mary Jo is saying that a long-term relationship is a gift. We need to feel we are worthy of it.

Intimacy: Knowing the Real Me

Intimacy is expressed, in part, through letting someone know you for who you truly are. It is also discovering who you truly are through someone else's knowing you.

I asked, "When you look at your relationship as a whole, what would you say are the most joyful things about it? What gives you the most pleasure?" Often the women's answers would have something to do with this kind of intimacy.

"We accept each other as we are." (Lori, age 41, 19-year couple)

"Being able to be totally myself without fear of judgment or criticism." (Margot, age 47, 10-year couple)

"It's wonderful to be free to be just who you are." (Suzanne, age 51, 19-year couple)

"I get enormous pleasure from the fact that my partner knows me so well." (Janet, age 52, 15-year couple)

"Having someone who knows me, with my myriad faults, who still loves and admires me (most of the time)." (Margery, age 71, 24-year couple)

"We are sincere and truthful; we are real to one another." (Sylvia, age 44, 10-year couple)

One woman describes her experience with this process of becoming "real" to your partner.

"Resolving crises is a struggle and a personal ordeal. A relationship like this — perhaps any relationship that lasts — is a fire which burns up parts of me and transmutes them. I am changed in the process, like the

Velveteen Rabbit; the fuzz gets rubbed off. The process holds a mirror to me all the time, and then asks me to polish myself." (Mary, age 39, 10-year couple)

This sense of being real to each other can be what ultimately holds us together. A woman reflects on why she didn't break up with her partner when she became attracted to someone else:

> "When things hit a critical point, I was forced to make a choice and discovered that I was unwilling to give up Libby. I think probably because I felt (and still feel) like she is the only person I have ever known who really knows me and loves me completely. The other woman was fun and sexually attractive, but didn't really know me." (Elaine, age 47, 17-year couple)

I believe this sense of "being real" to each other is a tremendously important motivation for lesbians, a motivation for being lesbians in the first place, and then perhaps for working to maintain and develop a long-term relationship with one other woman. Here I'm talking to a woman who was married for eight years before becoming a lesbian. She has been in her couple for thirteen years.

> *Susan:* Had you thought of yourself as just a regular straight person going through life like anybody else?
>
> *Deborah:* I knew something was not right, but I didn't know what it was. And then when

317

I met Kathy, all of a sudden I thought: this is it! It was like a wonderful coming home. Finally I understood how I wanted to live.

For some lesbians there is a pervasive sense of "faking it" in the heterosexual world.

Beverly was married for twenty-three years before becoming a lesbian. She is 58 years old, and her relationship is thirteen years along. Her partner Lauren is 47.

Beverly: There's not a hell of a lot of people that I know of who talk about their relationships that really trust the person that they're with. I mean totally. You know what I'm talkin' about. Where you don't feel embarrassed about having the person you're living with know about some of your weaknesses, some of your foibles. You don't have to maintain the front of appearance that is gonna be acceptable to someone. They know you at your best; they know you at your worst; they accept both.

Lauren: I know what you mean. Which is not to mean that you have to tell them everything.

Beverly: It means that you can exist with weaknesses that are obvious that they know about. I think that's one of the things that has made a lot of difference in our being together.

Susan: You mean it has made a lot of difference that you can give each other that?

Beverly: Especially for me. A lot of my life I lived very strong, very independent. I had a great big shell because I had to maintain this ability not to be hurt. And to be independent.

Lauren: You also lived a good part of your life on stage.

For many of us, being a lesbian means we can finally be who we really are. Then, being with one consistent partner can free us to develop who we really are to the point of being able to share our most intimate self with our partner. This process is a principal source of joy to the women in their long-term relationships.

Take Responsibility for Yourself

Talk of "who we really are" and "our most intimate self" brings us back to that awkwardly recurring subject, ourselves. This Self has been lurking throughout the pages of this book, peeping up now and then when we talk of having the courage to let go of one's self (commitment), or reveal one's self (sameness/differences), or enjoy one's self (sexuality), or extend one's self (family and friends). We met this Self straight on in the chapter on Problems where we found she caused a good many of the problems we would like to attribute to our partners.

Here are some final words on that slippery Self. Things seem to go better in couples if you can get your Self to:

1. *Tell the truth about yourself.*

Suzanne: I would say you can't give somebody advice on how to stay together, because staying together is the wrong focus; that's after the fact. First you have to be willing to grow and learn and be up front. I spent five years with Esther being afraid that if I said one thing that she didn't approve of, that I thought she would not like, she would leave me. That's a totally dependent point of view, and it doesn't work. If who I really am is not compatible with her, then I might as well find it out sooner than later, and go do something else. She kept saying that to me, but I'm hanging on for dear life trying to please. Because I'm so afraid.

When I finally let go of that, I found out what freedom is: that I can be who I am, she can be who she is, we can choose to live together, and we can work all the rest out after that.

Susan: Are you saying that staying together is a by-product? Something that happens as a result of doing all this other stuff you're talking about?

Suzanne: Yeah. Chances are if you fell in love, or have some bond, or really care about each other, then all the rest will work out. Then staying together isn't a by-product any more; it's the foundation. But you can't know that when you're trying to cope and adjust.

That's what's wrong with some therapy.

They just teach you how to cope and adjust. My experiences with therapists have all been cope and adjust kinds. I had to do the growing on my own.

Susan: You mean because when you're coping and adjusting you're trying to change yourself in order to be somebody you think your partner is gonna like?

Suzanne: Yeah. You're doing everything for a motive. The hardest thing in the world is to do something for no motive, and let the chips fall where they may. I didn't know that. And you can't explain it to anybody. You can't advise them how to be free.

Esther, Suzanne's partner, puts the same ideas this way when she says:

"Talk. Dare to be honest. Grow up, learn about yourself, become self-aware. Don't blame others, find your true self. And learn compassion!" (age 64)

2. *Focus on changing yourself, not your partner.*

Here a woman in a ten-year couple reflects on why this relationship has worked where others didn't.

"I have to look back on the 'failed' relationships of my past to find some of the explanation of why this one works for me. I brought a different set of expectations to this relationship, and that has made a difference.

"I'd had much of the romantic ideal

321

drubbed out of me in my just-previous five-year relationship. I came to a realization that to expect my fulfillment and happiness to be delivered to me in the form of my dream lover and her gifts to me was a script for disappointment, and gave away my power.

"I came to this realization with the knowledge that I make myself happy or not by what I bring to a situation, and how I choose to respond. It's not so clean cut as that sounds, but it was a real shift in me. Consequently I'm much more able than in the past to just let my lover be the person she is, to appreciate, enjoy, or dislike it as I will, but not to look to her to be some great fulfillment to me, like an infant looks to Mom.

"And, this relationship is much more satisfying than my past ones, at least partly, I think, because of this prior change in me." (Mary, age 39)

Here's the crux of the message about our Self and being a happy and fulfilled lesbian person: "Love yourself and do not be afraid." (Mary Lee, age 51, 22-year couple) I can't think how to say it any more clearly than that.

Joys, Pleasures

I feel confident in saying that the women in long-term lesbian couples do not persist in their relationships because they like to work so hard on interpersonal problems, or because they enjoy painful

322

self-revelation, or because they are curious to discover the benefits time can bestow upon them. They stay first and foremost because they are enjoying themselves, because — disillusionments and difficulties aside — their relationship is a source of pleasure to them.

And they're not stingy in praising their partners or letting us know how important their relationship is:

"She's still the love of my life and always will be. She's my hero." (Alice, age 53, 23-year couple)

"I love it! We are billionaires in love." (Debra, age 39, 15-year couple)

"It's the best thing that will ever happen to me. I consider it a gift for which I am truly thankful." (Kim, age 37, 18-year couple)

"My relationship is the base from which I view the world." (Judith, age 37, 13-year couple)

"I feel so blessed to be in this relationship. My lover is a wonderful person. I know her faults, but we have a good time." (Gail, age 60, 22-year couple)

Indeed, the women in long-term couples have a good time. I asked them about the sources of joy and pleasure in their lives together. Their responses group naturally around four themes:

1. *Appreciation of their partner:*

"I love holding and kissing her, making love, talking, and joking together. I just love spending time with her. I look forward to sharing time and my thoughts with her. When we're separated, nothing can be quite as much fun as when we can experience it together. She's the most interesting person I've ever met. I always learn from her." (Georgia, age 37, 15-year couple)

"She's a sweet, lovely person, a good soul. She moves me very deeply." (April, age 48, 14-year couple)

2. *Sharing life, being able to count on their partner:*

"I look forward to ending the day in each other's arms. An open, honest, loving and sharing of our lives, from the most important of decisions down to the smallest incident. There is always someone there, who cares and is willing to share it all (good or bad)." (Sheila, age 41, 13-year couple)

"Living with someone you love and trust. Someone that makes your life all it can be here on earth. It's wonderful to wake up each morning knowing you have someone to share your day with you." (Margaret, age 63, 23-year couple)

"That we are growing old *together*. That we have crossed many difficult times (family, illness) *together*. That we have each other." (Cecille, age 79, 45-year couple)

"The security of being number one." (Agnes, age 75, 41-year couple)

3. *Having fun together:*

"We both are still head over heels in love with the other! We both have a good sense of humor. We have mutual interests and appreciate the same things. We have fun with each other, and she's my best friend." (Peggy, age 42, 12-year couple)

"I feel our sexual relationship is very good. We feel comfortable in that area and have never experienced such pleasure with anyone else." (Sue, Peggy's partner, age 41)

"Above all humor! We break up at the same things. We both love reading and talking together about what we've read. We like nature and here on the island we feed our birds and watch the animals. We like to touch each other." (Sarah, age 60, 22-year couple)

"Silly things like watching the sunset, buying groceries, sex at halftime of the Sunday afternoon football game." (Jan, age 41, 25-year couple)

4. The ordinary pleasures of daily life:

"The ordinariness of our life. The everyday familiarity of getting up together, going to work, welcoming each other home after a time out with friends, fixing meals together, planning trips together, 'spooning up' for a while each night before we turn over and go to sleep." (Kathy, age 48, 13-year couple)

"I like the 'high points,' meeting new people together and doing new and interesting things, but the best is the bedrock: knowing she's there for me, sleeping with her every night, just being around each other, being at home together." (Betsy, age 39, 21-year couple)

"For me, it's seeing her make a long putt or hit a long drive, or make a small slam against good defense. Just the little things." (Gert, age 63, 25-year couple)

Some women incorporate all these themes; everything is a pleasure.

"Our love of music and dancing. Our ability to share feelings about most anything. Crying together over some cornball movie. Travelling together.

"Just our daily life together is generally pleasurable.

"I love her face, her voice, her body. She has opened up so much of the world for me, helped me relax and enjoy life. I'm quite crazy about her." (Donna, age 42, 11-year couple)

Ignore the Rules

We couldn't have become lesbians if following the rules were of paramount importance in our lives. In fact many women cannot become lesbians because they simply lack the courage; they are too afraid to contradict what society tells them and follow their own desires. We lesbians are risk-takers and rule-breakers in our core. Somewhere we found the courage.

What I want to suggest here is that we use that courage to ignore a few more rules.

"Risk-taking was not only important in the beginning, but it has been important all along: to consider new ways of thinking, behaving, deciding." (Tillie, age 41, 15-year couple)

In this case, the rules I want us to disregard come not only from the larger society, but from our friends and, most insidiously, from within ourselves.

The first rule we need to abandon is that if a relationship isn't happy all the time, it's no good and should be discarded for a new and different relationship. All the long-term couples know this is an idea lethal to longevity. You know why from having read this book. Kate (who has two children) sums it up. She's talking about sex here, but it could as well apply to a relationship in its entirety:

"Perfect sex is like perfect day-care or the perfect school or the perfect job; there's no such thing. You have to get beyond that. Once you do, it takes on a whole new dimension."

Thus: *Axiom 1: No relationship is perfect.*

The second rule to disregard is that there is one good way to live a relationship. I don't know a single long-term couple who believes this to be true. Instead they say,

"Be willing to let go of your ideals/beliefs about what ought/should/has to be. Get your 'old tapes' and ego out of the way, and be open to creating a relationship that is unique to yourselves. Listen to your own common sense and wisdom; make choices out of your happy, loving feelings instead of your insecurities." (Kathy, age 48, 13-year couple)

Your ego, of course, has to do with what we've been calling the Self. We all need to stop interfering with our own happiness, by abandoning having to be right, by letting our partner take care of us sometimes, by trusting, by growing up, by not confusing her with me. Whatever work you need to do on yourself will benefit your relationship enormously.

We think of "old tapes" as originating with our families of origin. Indeed, we do need to look closely at how our parents handled their relationship so we don't unthinkingly adopt their more destructive patterns simply because they're familiar. And we need to be humble enough to let their healthy ways of doing things influence us for the better.

But we need to beware of "new tapes," ideas that exist in the lesbian community — our adopted family — that may be just as destructive as those old tapes, or perhaps are simply inappropriate for us. The long-term couples are careful to warn us against being "politically correct."

> "Go with your heart. If you want to be in a long-term relationship, and the timing is right, it will probably work out. Don't feel pressured by 'shoulds,' either to stay with someone, or to have a politically-correct relationship." (Molly, age 38, 12-year couple)

The reason, of course, is that what is politically incorrect to one woman may be priceless to another. No one knows what you need better than yourself. And no one knows what you and your partner need from a relationship better than the two of you.

Axiom 2: There is no one perfect way to do a relationship.

Hopefully this book has shown you a variety of ways of being in a long-term lesbian relationship. You can feel committed for life; you can take it one day at a time. You can be merged; you can be separate. You can be affectionate and sexual; you can be affectionate and platonic. You can have chronic serious problems; your relationship can feel easy. You can love children and have them; you can loathe children and avoid them. You can be close to your families or distant. You can be part of the lesbian community or intentionally withdraw from it.

You can do any combination you want of any of these things to any degree you choose.

By being lesbians you have chosen an unusual path, one you believed would suit you, in fact would thrill you. Now you get to follow up on that first courageous step by designing the kind of relationship that will suit you both, that will fulfill you.

This is the odyssey of one couple, together twenty-five years. They became lovers when Beth was 14 and Karin 16. When I asked them "Have the things that have kept you together changed over the years?" Beth, now 39, said, "Yes":

"1. Originally, we stayed together because we were co-dependent and were afraid to do anything different;

"2. Then, because we learned to communicate our needs and how to fight without pushing the other person's most vulnerable buttons;

"3. Ultimately, because we came to realize that a relationship only has to meet the needs of the two people involved, not anyone else's expectations.

"And we learned to take care of ourselves, and to nurture each other."

This book has offered a lot of suggestions about what has worked for some couples and what hasn't. There's no dearth of examples and advice here. But it's still true that you can — in fact you must —

build your relationship any way you want, any way that feels good to the two of you.

What you can't do is expect your relationship to be static. Everything changes, and everything keeps changing.

Jane and Joanne are in their mid-fifties. They met in a swimming class in Cheyenne, Wyoming, thirty-one years ago.

> *Jane:* After reading my answers to this questionnaire again, it sounds as if we are sort of staggering, not growing anymore. This isn't true. I'm the first person to get bored with lack of growth and change. In all other facets of my life I have become a lover of change, adventure, and even foolhardiness. But for some reason I never get bored with my lover, nor do I cease learning things both from her and the world-at-large. She is less adventurous, but she also has grown and changed, especially the last ten years.
>
> If I keep writing, reading, walking, swimming, and travelling with her another thirty years, I'll remain the luckiest creature on Earth!

Like Rebecca (age 36, 15-year couple) says, "It's always a work in progress."

Bibliography

The following is a list of books I refer to plus a few others that are important in the field of same sex couples.

Bell, Alan P. and M.S. Weinberg. *Homosexualities: A Study of Diversity among Men and Women.* New York: Simon & Schuster, 1978.

Berzon, Betty. *Permanent Partners.* New York: E.P. Dutton, 1988.

Blumstein, Philip and Pepper Schwartz. *American Couples.* New York: Simon & Schuster, Pocket Books Edition, 1985. Originally published by William Morrow & Co., 1983.

Clunis, Merilee D. and G. Dorsey Green. *Lesbian Couples.* Seattle, WA: Seal Press, 1988.

Faderman, Lillian. *Suppressing the Love of Men.* New York: William Morrow & Co., 1981.

Klagsbrun, Francine. Married People. New York: Bantam Books, 1985.

McWhirter, David P. and Andrew M. Mattison. *The Male Couple.* Englewood Cliffs, NJ: Prentice-Hall, Inc., 1984.

Rich, Adrienne. "Compulsory Heterosexuality and Lesbian Existence," in *Signs,* 1980 (Vol. 5, No. 4), pages 631–660.

Sweet, James A. and Larry L. Bumpass. *American Families and Households.* New York: Russell Sage Foundation, 1987.

Tanner, Donna M. *The Lesbian Couple.* Lexington, MA: D.C. Heath & Co., 1978.